WAVERLY® at home
pillows

Meredith® Books
Des Moines, Iowa

Meredith® Press
An imprint of Meredith® Books

WAVERLY® At Home: Pillows

Editor: Vicki L. Ingham
Writer: Dondra Green Parham
Contributing Art Director: Marisa Dirks
Contributing Designer: Gayle Schadendorf
Copy Chief: Terri Fredrickson
Book Production Managers: Pam Kvitne, Marjorie J. Schenkelberg
Contributing Copy Editor: Carol Boker
Contributing Proofreaders: Becky Danley, Tricia Toney, Kathy Roth Eastman
Technical Readers: Margaret Sindelar, M. Peg Smith
Illustrator: Michael Burns
Indexer: Elizabeth T. Parson
Electronic Production Coordinator: Paula Forest
Editorial and Design Assistants: Kaye Chabot, Mary Lee Gavin, Karen Schirm

Meredith® Books
Editor in Chief: James D. Blume
Design Director: Matt Strelecki
Managing Editor: Gregory H. Kayko
Executive Decorating and Home Design Editor: Denise L. Caringer

Director, Retail Sales and Marketing: Terry Unsworth
Director, Sales, Special Markets: Rita McMullen
Director, Sales, Premiums: Michael A. Peterson
Director, Sales, Retail: Tom Wierzbicki
Director, Book Marketing: Brad Elmitt
Director, Operations: George A. Susral
Director, Production: Douglas M. Johnston

Vice President, General Manager: Jamie L. Martin
Meredith Publishing Group
President, Publishing Group: Stephen M. Lacy
Vice President, Finance and Administration: Max Runciman

Meredith Corporation
Chairman and Chief Executive Officer: William T. Kerr

Chairman of the Executive Committee: E. T. Meredith III

WAVERLY®

President: Christiane Michaels
Vice President, Marketing and Licensing: Carolyn A. D'Angelo
Director, Design, Licensed Product: Christina Angelides
Design Director, Licensing: Kristin Osterberg

Pillows do more than add comfort to chairs, sofas, and beds. They emphasize or accent the color scheme of a room, add variety to a palette of patterns and textures, and can even become focal points in a decorating scheme. Sewing your own pillows allows you to design accessories that express your personal style at a fraction of the cost of decorator pillows offered at interior design shops.

The projects in this book have been assigned skill levels and time requirements based on the following definitions:

Beginner: One who is familiar with basic sewing terms, such as seamline, seam allowance, grainline of fabric, and selvage edge. Experience with a sewing machine includes making seams, hemming, gathering, and installing zippers and welting. The beginner can work precisely from illustrations.

Intermediate: One who is comfortable with basic sewing terms and uses sewing techniques such as understitching and topstitching; can make custom paper patterns following written and illustrated instructions; has constructed a simple garment; and can make facings, install zippers, and make buttonholes.

Advanced: One who completely understands sewing terms and measurements; feels confident with the complexity of incorporating multiple elements in pillow construction; and easily makes paper pattern shapes from illustrations. Sewing experience includes details such as ruching.

The time required for each project is a general guide only; actual time required will depend on individual skill level and individual circumstances.

Please read all instructions carefully before beginning a project. If you encounter unfamiliar sewing terms in the instructions, please check the glossary on page 110 for help. On page 111, you will find a complete listing of the fabrics shown in the photos of each project.

table of contents

Fringe, welting, and other trims add personality and panache to basic pillows. Trims are usually sewn into the seam, but certain types may be applied to the surface for a richer effect.

basic pillows with trim

Pillows offer one of the easiest ways to accent the color scheme in a room. To play up a theme, use leftover fabric from draperies or upholstery to make two or three pillows; then choose two or more coordinating fabrics, such as checks, solids, and smaller or larger scaled prints, to make additional cushions. To avoid a too-perfectly matched effect, toss in one or two antique pillows that repeat the color theme.

Selecting a palette of coordinating fabrics is the first step. Next, add interest to your pillow collection with trims. Some trims, such as welting, cording with a lip, or moss fringe, are sewn into the seam. Other braids and fringes are applied to the surface of the pillow along the edge. (For more information, see pages 10–11.)

To unify a variety of fabrics, use the same color trim on all the pillows. The red check pillow *at left* is trimmed in short brush fringe sewn into the seam. Tassel fringe applied to the front finishes the floral pillow. The green pillow is edged with a pairing of welting and tassel fringe in the seam.

basic pillow with welt edge:

1 From fabric, cut 2 (19") squares for front and back panels. Also cut enough 1½"-wide bias strips to make 2¼ yards. Stitch the bias strips together at the short ends to make 1 continuous length.

2 To make welting, fold the bias strip, wrong sides together, around the filler cord, matching the long raw edges. Using a zipper foot and a long stitch length, baste close to the cord, encasing the cord in the fabric (see Figure 1).

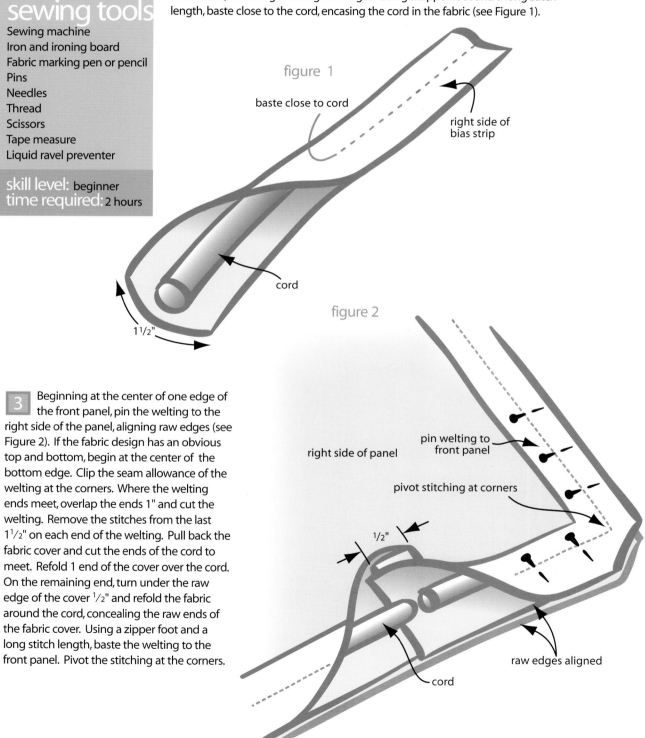

figure 1

baste close to cord

right side of
bias strip

cord

1½"

figure 2

3 Beginning at the center of one edge of the front panel, pin the welting to the right side of the panel, aligning raw edges (see Figure 2). If the fabric design has an obvious top and bottom, begin at the center of the bottom edge. Clip the seam allowance of the welting at the corners. Where the welting ends meet, overlap the ends 1" and cut the welting. Remove the stitches from the last 1½" on each end of the welting. Pull back the fabric cover and cut the ends of the cord to meet. Refold 1 end of the cover over the cord. On the remaining end, turn under the raw edge of the cover ½" and refold the fabric around the cord, concealing the raw ends of the fabric cover. Using a zipper foot and a long stitch length, baste the welting to the front panel. Pivot the stitching at the corners.

pin welting to
front panel

pivot stitching at corners

right side of panel

½"

raw edges aligned

cord

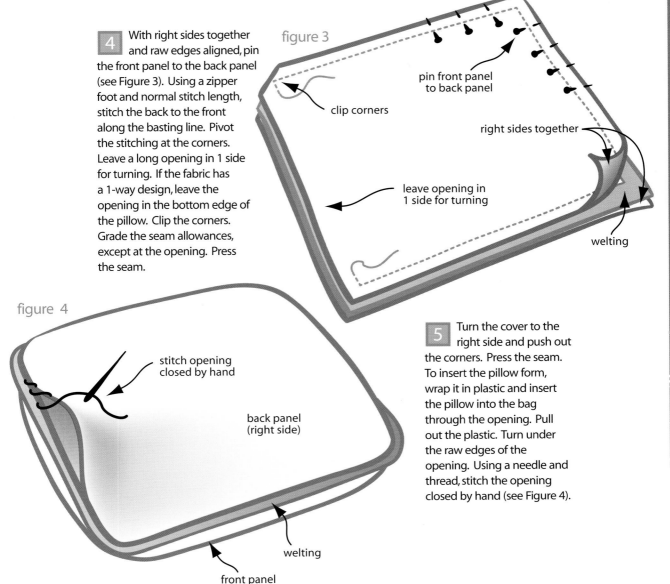

4 With right sides together and raw edges aligned, pin the front panel to the back panel (see Figure 3). Using a zipper foot and normal stitch length, stitch the back to the front along the basting line. Pivot the stitching at the corners. Leave a long opening in 1 side for turning. If the fabric has a 1-way design, leave the opening in the bottom edge of the pillow. Clip the corners. Grade the seam allowances, except at the opening. Press the seam.

figure 3

pin front panel to back panel

clip corners

right sides together

leave opening in 1 side for turning

welting

figure 4

stitch opening closed by hand

back panel (right side)

welting

front panel

5 Turn the cover to the right side and push out the corners. Press the seam. To insert the pillow form, wrap it in plastic and insert the pillow into the bag through the opening. Pull out the plastic. Turn under the raw edges of the opening. Using a needle and thread, stitch the opening closed by hand (see Figure 4).

PICKING THE PERFECT PILLOW FORM

■ Pillow forms provide the easiest way to create an evenly stuffed cushion. Purchase these prestuffed cushions at fabric centers, discount stores, and home decorating fabric stores. The forms come in a range of standard sizes, the most common being 14", 16", 18", and 24" squares. Specialty shapes, such as neckroll and boudoir pillow forms, are also available.

■ The forms generally have a white or off-white cotton cover and come filled with one of a variety of materials. Down-filled cushions are extremely soft and sumptuous, but down does not hold its form well with heavy use. Feather/down-filled forms mimic the softness of down-only forms, but provide more stability and hold their shape better. The

material in the feather/down pillow is usually 95 percent feather and 5 percent down. The feather content supports the pillow shape under day-to-day use, and the down provides the slouchy softness.

■ Fiber-filled pillow forms create firm, springy pillows. These are usually the least expensive forms available. The polyester filling is distributed evenly inside the cotton cover for a smooth shape with no lumps or bumps. Choose fiber-filled pillows for use in children's rooms or any location where you need a pillow that can take heavy use. If you want to make a rectangular or round pillow or a square in a size other than the standard ones, you can stitch your own cover from muslin and stuff it with polyester fiberfill.

PASSEMENTERIE

■ Fringe, braid, cording, and welting are all types of passementerie, a French term for fancy trims that add texture and color to pillows, draperies, and upholstery. Whether you choose a tassel fringe over a ball fringe is a matter of personal taste, but the material from which the trim is made does affect its character. Ball fringe in brightly colored cotton has a playful look, for example, while the same type of fringe in richly hued rayon is formal and elegant.

■ Trims designed for application to the surface of a pillow have a decorative braid or band that holds the fringe or trim elements together. Other types of trim, intended to be stitched into the seam in the same manner as welting, have a plain braid or lip. You insert the lip into the seam and stitch it in place as you assemble the pillow. Ball fringe, cording with a lip, many styles of tassel fringe, and brush or moss fringe fit this category.

TECHNIQUES MADE EASY

surface application of trims: Invisible thread is the key to stitching trims to pillow fronts.

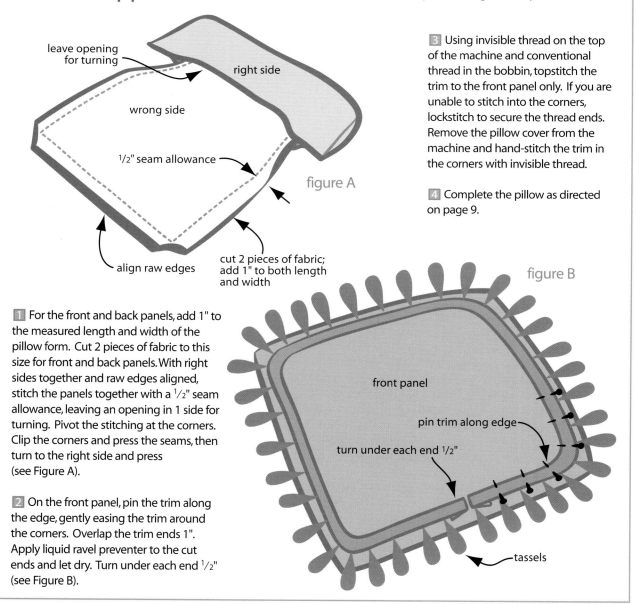

leave opening for turning

right side

wrong side

1/2" seam allowance

figure A

align raw edges

cut 2 pieces of fabric; add 1" to both length and width

front panel

pin trim along edge

turn under each end 1/2"

figure B

tassels

3 Using invisible thread on the top of the machine and conventional thread in the bobbin, topstitch the trim to the front panel only. If you are unable to stitch into the corners, lockstitch to secure the thread ends. Remove the pillow cover from the machine and hand-stitch the trim in the corners with invisible thread.

4 Complete the pillow as directed on page 9.

1 For the front and back panels, add 1" to the measured length and width of the pillow form. Cut 2 pieces of fabric to this size for front and back panels. With right sides together and raw edges aligned, stitch the panels together with a 1/2" seam allowance, leaving an opening in 1 side for turning. Pivot the stitching at the corners. Clip the corners and press the seams, then turn to the right side and press (see Figure A).

2 On the front panel, pin the trim along the edge, gently easing the trim around the corners. Overlap the trim ends 1". Apply liquid ravel preventer to the cut ends and let dry. Turn under each end 1/2" (see Figure B).

in-seam application of trims:

Stitching the trim into the seam is the most common way of accenting the edges of a pillow.

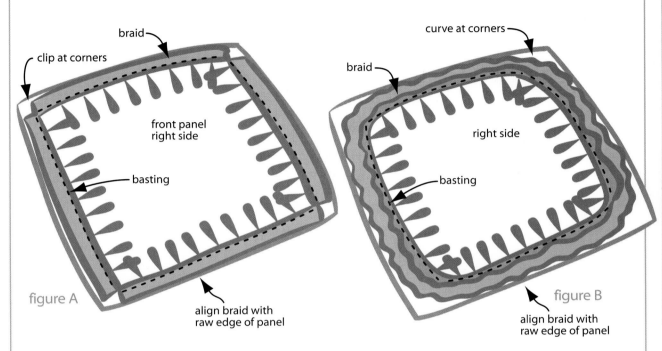

figure A — clip at corners — braid — front panel right side — basting — align braid with raw edge of panel

figure B — curve at corners — braid — right side — basting — align braid with raw edge of panel

1 Measure the width of the braid or the lip on the trim. Double this measurement and add it to the width and length of the pillow form. From fabric, cut 2 pieces this size for front and back panels.

2 On the right side of the front panel, align the braid or lip with the raw edges of the panel so the fringe or cording extends toward the center of the panel. Pin in place, clipping the braid or lip at the corners. Apply liquid ravel preventer to the cut edges and let dry. (Although not shown in the drawing, where the ends of the trim meet, they should overlap 1/2".) Apply liquid ravel preventer to the cut ends and let dry. Using a long stitch length, baste the trim to the panel along the inside edge of the braid or lip (see Figure A).

3 For thick or heavy trims, such as brush fringe, gently round each corner. (Although not shown in the drawing,

where the ends of the trim meet, they should overlap 1/2".) Turn the final few sections of fringe into the seam allowance. Baste the fringe to the panel along the inside edge of the bound edge of the fringe (see Figure B).

4 With right sides together and raw edges aligned, follow the previous basting line to stitch the front panel to the back panel, catching the lip in the stitches. Stitch the panels together on 3 sides; stitch all corners, pivoting at square corners and working in a continuous curve on rounded corners. Leave an opening in 1 side for turning. Grade the seams and clip the corners. Press the seams and turn to the right side. Press the seams.

5 Insert the pillow form as directed on page 9. Turn the raw edges of the opening to the inside and stitch the opening closed by hand.

Slipcovers transform chairs and sofas—why not pillows? Layering fabrics, such as a coordinating solid or print, over the pillow's cover adds richness and can shift the color emphasis in the room. The red check on the pillow *opposite*, for example, plays up the warmth of the color scheme. A blue slipcover would make the blue elements in the fabrics more prominent.

pillow with tie-on slipcover

The creative possibilities are nearly endless with easy-to-sew pinafore-like covers. Make the pillows with covers that coordinate to take advantage of the benefits of layering, or stitch covers to perk up the knife-edge pillows you keep around all year.

To freshen dated-looking pillows, choose a fabric in a color that coordinates or contrasts with the fabric on the pillow. On the one *opposite*, for example, a white cotton slipcover would give the pillow a summertime look, while a blue gingham pinafore would emphasize the blue in the sofa upholstery and cool down the color scheme.

You also can use slipcovers to bring a sense of the changing seasons indoors. For spring and summer, choose white cotton or linen. For winter, create a cozy look with dark plaids, deep paisley patterns, or rich solids in felt, wool, and flannel. And for the holidays, make pinafores from velvet, organdy, or holiday-print fabrics for a festive, elegant accent.

FAST FACTS ON FUSIBLE WEB

■ You don't need a sewing machine to make pillow pinafores. Simply use paper-backed fusible adhesive tape and an iron to secure the hems. Tack ribbon ties to the slipcover with a few hand stitches.

■ Paper-backed fusible adhesive material makes easy work of other home decorating projects too. Use it to bond fabric to other porous materials, such as paper lampshades.

■ It generally takes two steps to fuse fabrics. First apply the paper-backed fusible adhesive material to one fabric with a hot iron. Remove the paper backing. Next, place the fabric as desired—turn the hem, for example—and fuse the layers together.

■ Read the manufacturer's instructions for fabric suitability. Some recommend different weights of fusible material depending on the fabric you will be using.

14"-square pillow form
$1/2$ yard 54"-wide decorator fabric
$1/2$ yard 54"-wide complementary decorator fabric

sewing tools

Sewing machine
Iron and ironing board
Fabric marking pen or pencil
Pins
Needles
Thread
Scissors
Tape measure
Liquid ravel preventer

skill level: beginner
time required: 3½ hours

pillow with tie-on slipcover:

1 To make the pillow, from fabric, cut 2 (15") squares for the front and back panels. If the fabric has a prominent design, match the pattern from the front panel to the back panel on as many edges as possible.

2 With right sides together, raw edges aligned and patterns matching, stitch the front panel to the back, using a $1/2$" seam allowance. Pivot the stitching at the corners and stitch all corners, leaving an opening in 1 side for turning. Clip the corners and press the seam. Turn the cover to the right side and press the seam.

3 Wrap the pillow form in plastic. Insert the form into the cover, then remove the plastic. Turn the raw edges of the opening to the inside. Using a needle and thread, stitch the opening closed by hand.

4 To make the slipcover, from complementary fabric, cut 2 ($15^{1}/_{2}$"×18") pieces for front and back panels. Cut 4 (2"×12") ties. Set the ties aside.

5 With right sides together and raw edges aligned, pin the front panel to the back panel on both 18" sides and on one $15^{1}/_{2}$" side. Using a $1/2$" seam allowance, stitch the panels on the pinned edges. Clip the corners and press the seam. Turn to the right side and press the seam.

6 On the open edge of the cover, turn the raw edges under $1/4$" twice. Press. Edgestitch along the fold to finish the edge. Measure and mark a line $2^{1}/_{2}$" from the finished edge. Fold the fabric to the right side along the marked line (see Figure 1). Press to crease. Set aside.

7 With wrong sides together, fold each tie in half, matching the long edges. Press to crease, then open the fold. On 1 short end, turn under $1/2$" and press (see Figure 2). Turn each long edge to meet the center crease. Press. Refold the center crease. Topstitch through all layers along the folded short end and the long edge of the tie. Press.

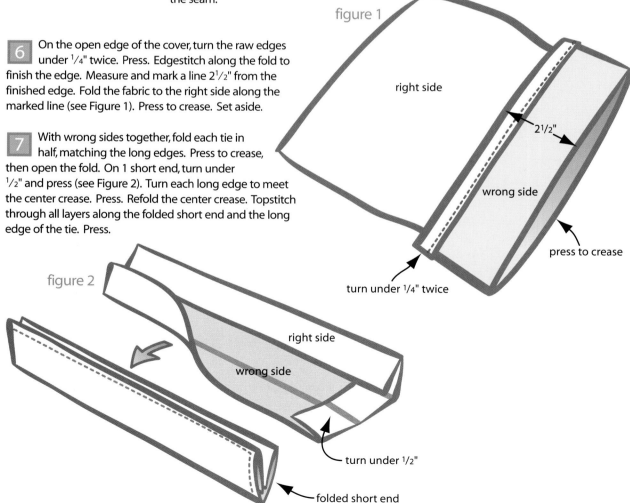

figure 1

right side

wrong side

$2^{1}/_{2}$"

press to crease

turn under $1/4$" twice

figure 2

right side

wrong side

turn under $1/2$"

folded short end

8 On the open edge of the cover, measure 3½" from each side seam, marking a point on both the front and back panels. At each marked point, insert the raw end of 1 tie into the fold on the open edge of the cover (see Figure 3). Stitch ½" from the fold of the open edge, catching the ties in the stitching line.

9 Press the seam and open the fold. Press. Turn the finished edge of the opening to the inside of the cover to make the facing. Place the seam with the ties on the edge and match the side seams of the cover and the facing. To secure the facing on the open edge, stitch in the ditch along each side seam.

10 Insert the finished pillow into the cover. Make bows with the pairs of ties to close the slipcover opening.

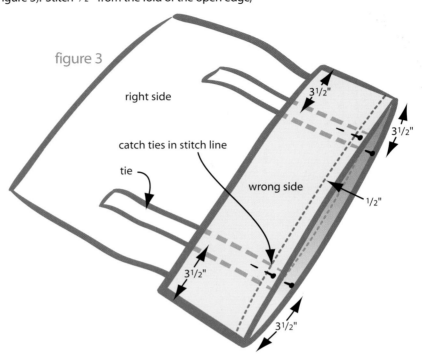

figure 3

right side

catch ties in stitch line

tie

3½"

3½"

wrong side

½"

3½"

3½"

MORE GOOD IDEAS

creative closures: Add style and personality to pillow slipcovers by choosing unusual closures.

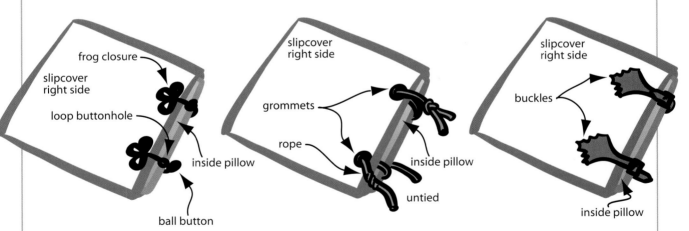

frog closure

slipcover right side

loop buttonhole

inside pillow

ball button

slipcover right side

grommets

rope

inside pillow

untied

slipcover right side

buckles

inside pillow

A Frog closures give the slipcover a look of formal elegance. Stitch the loop to the back panel and the three-looped closure to the front panel. Make sure the two pieces are perfectly aligned so the slipcover lies straight on the pillow when you insert the button through the loop.

B For a more casual effect, use large grommets and rope, twine, or leather thongs. This kind of closure would suit a slipcover made of canvas or muslin and would work well for pillows used outdoors on a porch or deck. Grommet closures also work in a child's room or informal family room.

C Use buckles to secure a slipcover made from wool plaid, corduroy, or canvas to use in a child's room, a den, or a playroom. These buckles are actually kilt tabs. Check the notions aisle at your local fabric center to find them. Secure the buckle ends with fabric glue or machine-stitch in place.

Use remnants from drapery or upholstery projects to create your own pillows that tie together your room's pattern palette. It's an easy technique for showing off special textiles.

creative custom fabrics

Repeating fabric elements within a room unifies the design. In this room, for example, the fabric in the window treatment appears on the upholstered seat of the side chairs and on the sofa pillows. However, the pillows don't display the fabric in full; instead, they accent a portion of the striped floral.

Combining motifs from fabrics or from portions of related fabrics to create a new textile underscores the palette of patterns, colors, and textures you've chosen for the room. Use remnants from larger projects, such as a window treatment, to make strips to embellish a pillow front.

In this project, the width of the appliqué pieces is determined by the width of the floral stripe featured at the center of the pillow. If you are working with an all-over design, plan for the three appliqué strips to be of equal width, or arrange them symmetrically if they are of unequal width. The complete design should cover approximately one-half to two-thirds of the total width of the pillow front.

creative custom fabrics:

1 From the main pillow fabric, cut 2 (17") squares for the front and back panels. Cut 1 (2"×17") strip for the zipper flap. If working with a fabric design that has an obvious top and bottom, cut the zipper flap to match the lower edge of the back panel. From accent fabric (the floral stripe in the sample pillow), cut out 1 strip to the desired width, adding 1/4" allowance on each long edge. To make it easier to design the pillow front, leave some excess length on the strip: This will allow you to position the motifs in the stripe as you desire. From a second accent fabric (a check in the sample pillow), cut 2 (17"-long) strips the measured width of the first accent strip plus 1".

2 On the front panel, arrange the accent fabrics, centering the arrangement. Place gimp over the long raw edges of the stripe piece to visualize the finished effect. Measure from the side edge of the pillow front to the edge of the check fabric and add 1/2" for the placement line of the check accent. Remove the accent fabrics from the front panel.

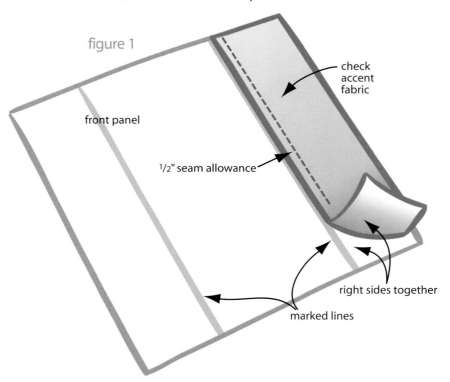

figure 1

check accent fabric

front panel

1/2" seam allowance

right sides together

marked lines

3 Measure from each side edge of the front panel and mark lines for the placement of the check accents (see Figure 1). With right sides together, align 1 raw edge of 1 check accent strip with each marked line, allowing the accent strips to extend beyond the side edges of the front panel. Using a 1/2" seam allowance on the check, stitch the check accent strips to the panel along the marked lines (see Figure 1). Press the seam. Turn the check accent strips toward the center of the front panel. Press.

4 Center the floral stripe piece on the front panel, covering the raw edges of the check accents. Zigzag over each long raw edge of the floral stripe piece, stitching through the check fabric and the front panel. Trim the ends of the floral strip even with the front panel.

5 Place gimp over each raw edge of the center strip. Thread the top of the machine with invisible thread and load conventional thread on the bobbin. Using a long stitch length, topstitch the gimp to the front panel on each long edge of the floral piece (see Figure 2). Stitch each edge of the gimp in the same direction, rather than stitching down 1 edge and up the other. This will alleviate puckering in the finished front panel. Turn the panel to the wrong side. Press the stitches.

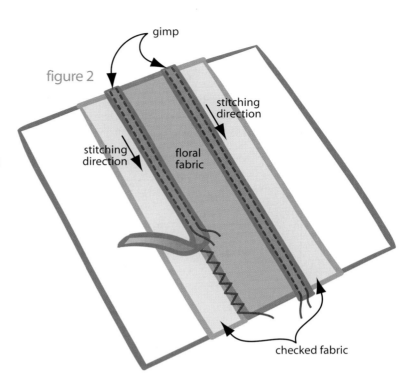

figure 2

gimp

stitching direction

stitching direction

floral fabric

checked fabric

6 On the right side of the front panel, align the braid of the tassel fringe with the raw edges of the panel and lay the fringe toward the center of the panel. Pin in place. Clip the braid at the corners. Where the braid ends meet, overlap the ends ¹/₂". Apply liquid ravel preventer to the cut ends and edges and let it dry. Using a long stitch length, baste the trim to the panel along the inside edge of the braid. Press the panel on the wrong side. Set the front panel aside.

7 Lay the back panel and the zipper flap right side up. Center the zipper facedown on the top long edge of the zipper flap (see Figure 3). Align the zipper tape with the raw edge of the flap. Using the zipper foot, stitch the zipper tape to the zipper flap. Turn the zipper faceup and press the seam.

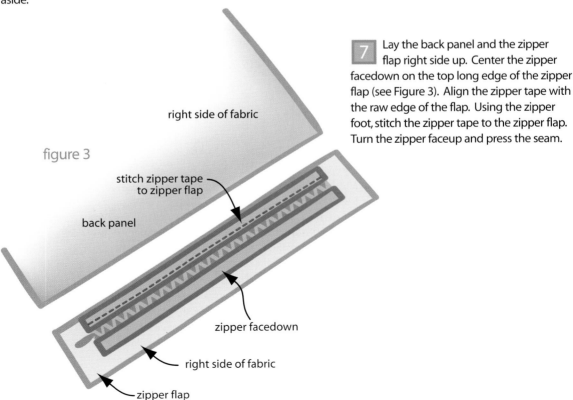

right side of fabric

figure 3

stitch zipper tape to zipper flap

back panel

zipper facedown

right side of fabric

zipper flap

8 On the bottom edge of the back panel, turn under 1¼" and press. Open the fold. Center the zipper on the bottom raw edge, aligning the raw edge of the fabric with the zipper tape (see Figure 4). Using a zipper foot, stitch the zipper tape to the edge. Press.

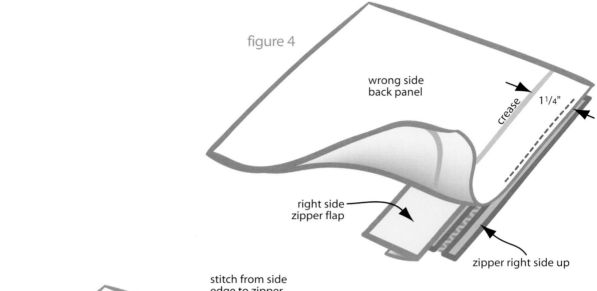

figure 4

wrong side
back panel

crease

1¼"

right side
zipper flap

zipper right side up

figure 5

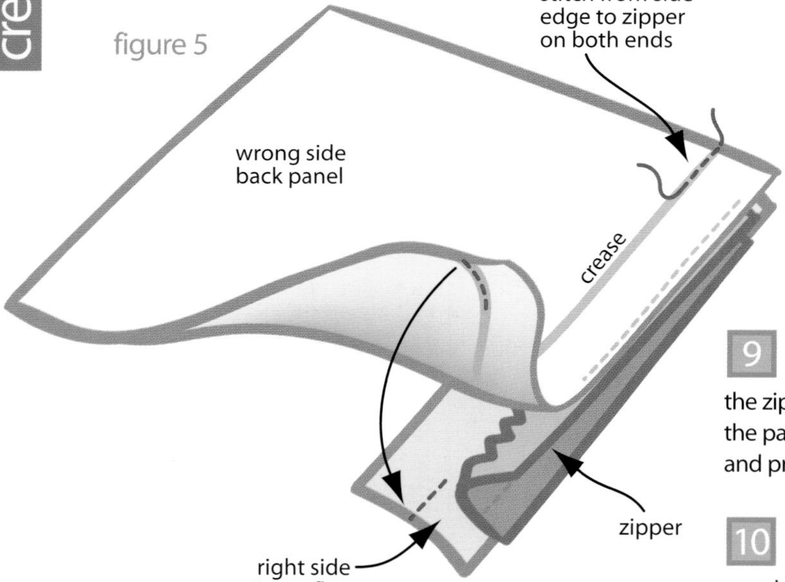

stitch from side
edge to zipper
on both ends

wrong side
back panel

crease

right side
zipper flap

zipper

9 With the fold in the bottom edge of the back panel open, stitch the crease to the zipper flap at both ends of the zipper (see Figure 5). Begin stitching at the side edges of the panel and stop stitching at the zipper. Refold the crease and press.

10 Compare the zippered back panel to the front panel. If necessary, trim the bottom edge of the zippered back panel to match the size of the front panel. Open the zipper. With right sides together and raw edges aligned, stitch the back panel to the front panel along the previous basting line on the front panel. Pivot the stitching at the corners. Clip the corners. Apply liquid ravel preventer to the cut edges of the braid and let dry. Press the seam.

11 Turn to the right side through the zipper. Reach inside the cover to push out the corners. Cover the seam and fringe with a pressing cloth. Press the seam from the right side. Insert the pillow form into the cover.

one-of-a-kind pillows
Combine techniques and materials to make your own designer pillows.

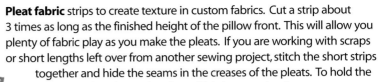

gimp

Pleat fabric strips to create texture in custom fabrics. Cut a strip about 3 times as long as the finished height of the pillow front. This will allow you plenty of fabric play as you make the pleats. If you are working with scraps or short lengths left over from another sewing project, stitch the short strips together and hide the seams in the creases of the pleats. To hold the pleats in place, baste the pleated fabric to a strip of nonwoven interfacing. Cover the pleats with a press cloth soaked in a solution of 1 cup water and $1/4$ cup distilled white vinegar; press firmly. The vinegar press makes the pleats permanent.

pleated fabric

tassel fringe

Appliqué a motif from one fabric onto another to combine two designs. Apply paper-backed fusible adhesive material to the wrong side of the appliqué fabric, following the manufacturer's instructions. Cut out the motif or design. Remove the paper backing and fuse the motif to the front panel of the pillow. Use a satin stitch to cover all the cut edges of the appliqué. To add dimension to the motif, consider accenting portions of the design with satin stitching.

appliqué

satin stitch edges

fringe

welting

fabric panel

stitch in the ditch

Create a **fabric badge** by framing a small fabric panel with a combination of trims, such as a loop fringe with a sculpted or scalloped edge and welting made from a complementary fabric. Place the badge, (the fabric-and-trim unit) at the center of the front panel. Stitch in the ditch between the fabric and the welting to secure the badge to the front panel.

why worry about directional stitching?

Why does it matter in which direction you stitch when applying braid or trim to a pillow? The feed dog on the sewing machine pulls the fabric under the needle as you stitch. If you stitch down one side of a trim, then turn the fabric around to stitch up the other, the feed dog will rumple the fabric on the underside of the trim. The result is a trim that twists or pulls out of shape and fabric that lumps.

To avoid this, stitch along each side of the trim in the same direction. Identify one end of the trim as the starting point and place this end under the machine first. When you reach the end, cut the threads and return to the starting point to stitch the remaining side. This way, the trim will lie flat on the fabric.

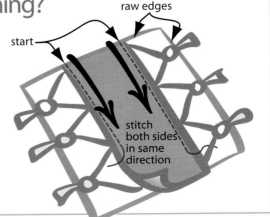

raw edges

start

stitch both sides in same direction

The secret to turning an ordinary striped fabric into a custom-designed pillow, such as the one shown *at left*, is to make a pattern that helps you line up the stripes before you sew. Stitch an invisible zipper into one of the edge seams to make the cover removable for laundering or dry cleaning.

mitered stripe pillow

To make the pattern for matching stripes to make mitered seams, use tracing paper, which will allow you to see the exact pattern placement on the fabric. With accurate cutting, the pieces will fit together beautifully—and if there is a slight mismatch at the center, simply hide it (and accent the pillow) with a tassel or decorative medallion.

The advantage to using an invisible zipper is that no topstitching shows on the right side of the pillow cover. The zipper coils will be hidden in the seam, leaving only a small zipper pull dangling from the seam.

Invisible zippers work best when no welting or trim is inserted in the seam between the front and back panels. If you are working with soft, thin fabrics, such as taffeta or silk dupioni, you can (with some practice) insert an invisible zipper into the seam with welting, tassel or ball fringe, or a ruffle.

materials

18"-square pillow form
1 yard 54"-wide striped
   decorator fabric
14" invisible zipper
Tracing paper

sewing tools

Sewing machine
Iron and ironing board
Fabric marking pen or pencil
Pins
Needles
Thread
Scissors
Tape measure
Liquid ravel preventer

skill level: intermediate
time required: 4½ hours

mitered stripe pillow:

1 From tracing paper, cut an 18" square (the same size as the pillow form). Fold the square from corner to corner on the diagonal. Crease. Open the square and fold on the opposite diagonal. Crease. Open the square and cut along the creases to make 4 identical triangle patterns.

2 Place 1 pattern on the fabric to determine the desired placement of the fabric design on the pillow. For the pillow shown on page 22, the green stripe bordered on either side by a red stripe is the center stripe in the pillow piece. When the 4 pieces are combined, this stripe will form a cross at the pillow center and the remaining stripes will make chevrons along the seams.

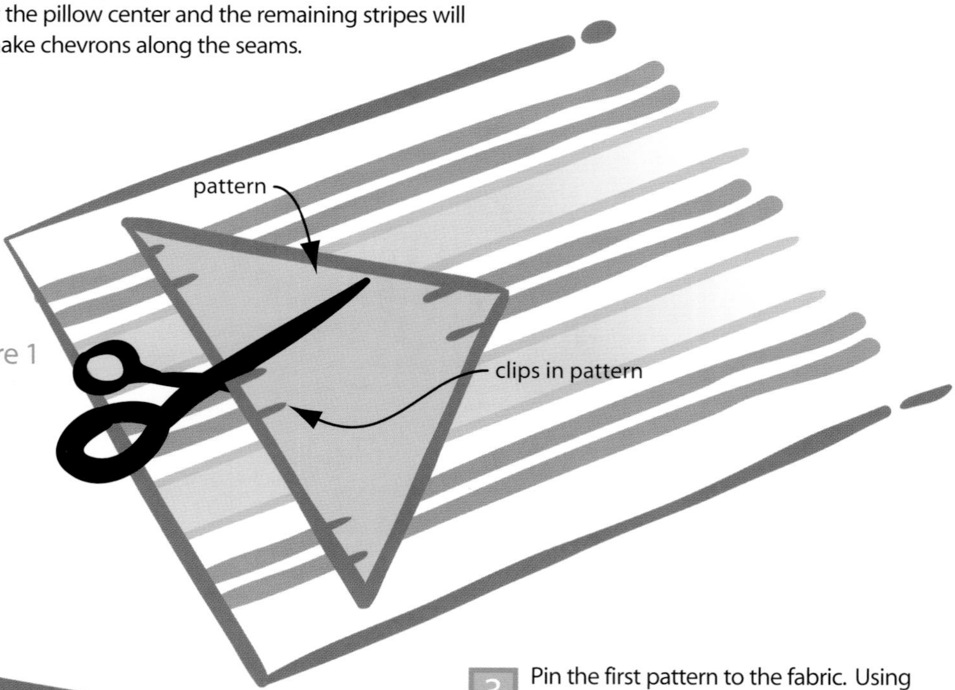

pattern

clips in pattern

figure 1

3 Pin the first pattern to the fabric. Using scissors, make small clips within the seam allowance in the pattern to mark the placement of the stripes (see Figure 1).

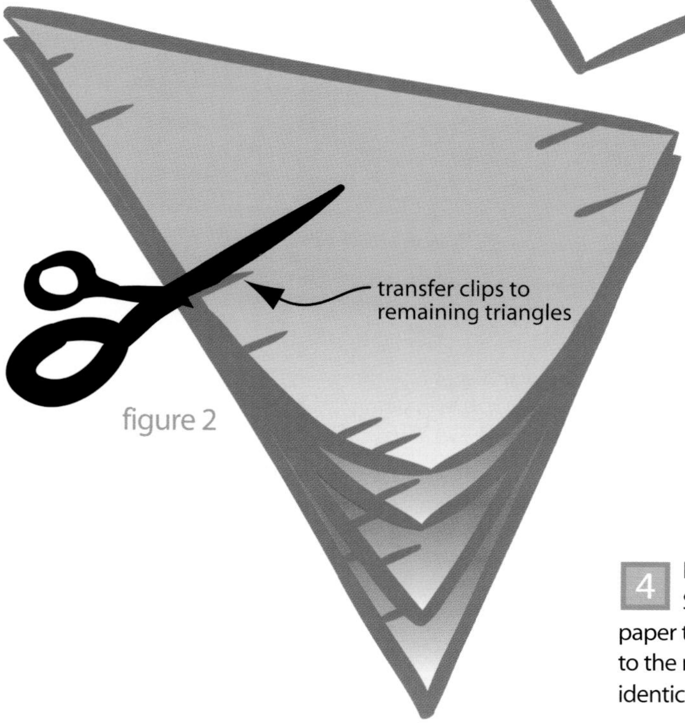

transfer clips to remaining triangles

figure 2

4 Remove the pattern from the fabric. Stack the first pattern on the remaining paper triangles. Transfer the clips to the remaining triangles to make identical patterns.

5 Pin each pattern on a single layer of fabric, matching the stripes to the clips in the edges of the pattern. Inspect the pattern placement to make sure each fabric piece will be identical. Mark a $1/2$" seam allowance around all edges of each pattern piece. Cut out on the marked lines to produce 4 triangle pieces.

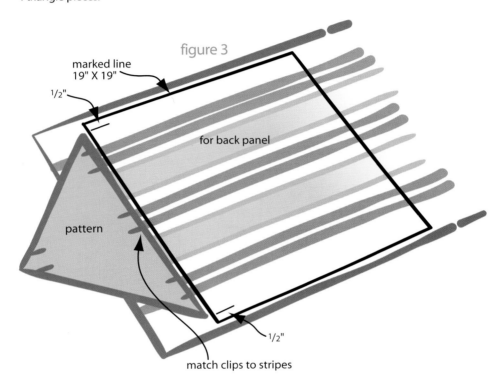

figure 3

marked line 19" X 19"

$1/2$"

for back panel

pattern

$1/2$"

match clips to stripes

6 For the back panel, place 1 pattern section on the fabric, matching the clips to the stripes in the fabric (see Figure 3). On the fabric, mark a line $1/2$" beyond each end of the long edge of the pattern. Using the marked lines as a guide, cut a 19" square. Set the back panel aside.

7 With the right sides together and raw edges aligned, pin 2 pairs of triangular pieces together on one diagonal edge, matching the stripes. Using a $1/2$" seam allowance, stitch the pieces together on the pinned edge. Stitch the remaining pair of triangles together on 1 edge in the same manner. Check the seams for the alignment of the stripes. Press the seams open.

mitered stripe pillow continued

8 With right sides together and raw edges aligned, pin the long edges of the resulting triangles together, matching the stripes and center seam. Using a $1/2$" seam allowance, stitch the pieces together. Check the seam for the alignment of the stripes. Press the seam open. If the seams don't quite match at the center, add a tassel or button over the intersection.

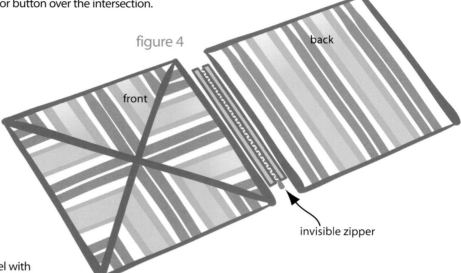

figure 4

front

back

invisible zipper

9 Lay the front panel and back panel with right sides face up. Arrange the panels side by side (see Figure 4). Insert the zipper in this seam, where you do not need to match the stripes across the seam. Center the invisible zipper, tab side up between the panels. Follow the manufacturer's instructions to install the zipper, centering it on each fabric edge. Do not stitch the ends of the seam together at this time.

10 With right sides together and raw edges aligned, pin the side edges of the front panel to the back panel, matching the stripes. Using a $1/2$" seam allowance, stitch the pinned edges together. Check the alignment of the stripes. Press the seams open, then turn to the right side and press.

11 Turn to the wrong side. With right sides together and raw edges aligned, pin the seams at each end of the zipper. Using a $1/2$" seam allowance and zipper foot, stitch the ends of the seam. Press the seam open. Open the zipper. With right sides together and raw edges aligned, pin the remaining open edge of the panels together (the edge opposite the zipper). Using a $1/2$" seam allowance, stitch the front panel to the back panel on the pinned edge. Press the seams open.

12 Clip the corners, then turn to the right side through the zipper. Press the seams. Using a needle and thread, stitch the tassel by hand to the center front of the cover where the seams intersect. Insert the pillow form into the cover and close the zipper.

designing with mitered seams:
Change the placement of the pattern pieces to yield a variety of effects.

Concentric Squares: Change the layout of the pattern pieces to create a pillow front of concentric squares. By placing the long side of the paper triangles along the stripe, you create boxes of graduated size on the pillow front.

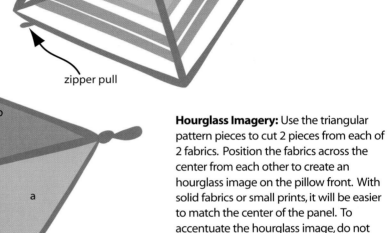

zipper pull

Hourglass Imagery: Use the triangular pattern pieces to cut 2 pieces from each of 2 fabrics. Position the fabrics across the center from each other to create an hourglass image on the pillow front. With solid fabrics or small prints, it will be easier to match the center of the panel. To accentuate the hourglass image, do not sew a button or tassel to the center of the panel.

zipper pull

Faux Wrap: Cut 2 pairs of triangles from each of two contrasting fabrics. Arrange the fabric pairs on opposite sides of the square to make an hourglass shape. From the remaining fabric, cut 2 (12"-long by 3"-wide) lozenge-shape pieces. With right sides together and raw edges aligned, stitch the pieces together, using a 1/4" seam allowance. Pivot the stitching at the points. Leave an opening in 1 side for turning. Press the seam and clip the corners and curves, then turn to the right side and place the seam on the edge. Turn the raw edges at the opening to the inside and press. Stitch the opening closed by hand. Make a knot at the center of the piece and stitch the knot to the center of the front of the pillow.

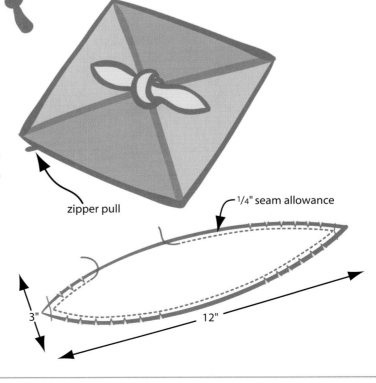

zipper pull

1/4" seam allowance

3"

12"

mitered stripe pillow how-to

Piece of souvenir textile
Pillow form
¾ yard 54"-wide decorator
    fabric
½ yard 54"-wide accent fabric
14" invisible zipper

sewing tools

Sewing machine
Thread
Pins
Needles
Scissors
Tape measure
Liquid ravel preventer
Fabric marking pen or pencil
Iron and ironing board

skill level: advanced
time required: 4 hours

mitered borders:

Use the technique of mitering to make borders for framing a special piece of fabric. A souvenir from your travels, such as a small purse or a scarf embroidered in a traditional design, could become the centerpiece of a one-of-a-kind pillow when framed with a border. Vintage fabrics or scraps of old textiles can be used this way too.

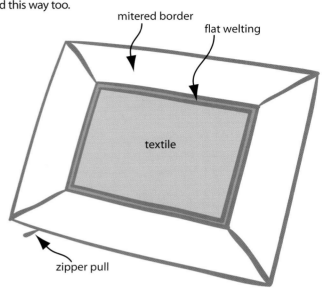

1 Fold or cut the textile to the desired size for the pillow top's center panel, adding ½" on each edge for the seam allowance. You will custom-fit the mitered border to the size of the center panel. Choose a pillow form with proportions similar to those of the textile but larger. Cut a piece of paper the same size as the pillow form.

2 Center the textile on the paper and lightly trace around the textile's edges. Remove the textile and boldly mark a line ½" inside the traced edge of the textile to show the placement of the center panel (see Figure 1). Mark the top, bottom, right, and left sides of the paper to identify the pattern pieces you will make later. Lay a ruler from each marked corner of the center panel to the paper's corresponding outside corner and draw a line. Cut the paper along the lines at the corners and the bold lines at the center to make 4 border templates; discard the center.

3 Use the paper pieces as templates for the border pieces. On the right side of the border fabric, place each template with the labeled side face up. Pin. Measure and mark a cutting line ½" from each edge of the template. Cut the border pieces on the marked lines.

4 Measure the pillow form from the top to the bottom and add 1". Measure the pillow form from side to side and add 1". Cut 1 pillow back from fabric to this size.

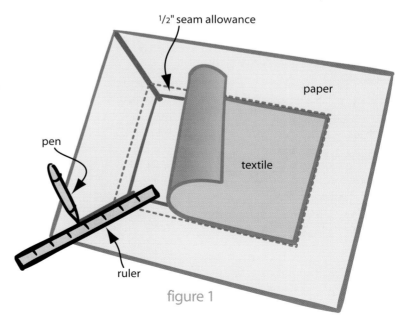

figure 1

5 From the accent fabric, cut enough 1½"-wide bias strips to equal 2 yards and stitch the strips together at the short ends to make a continuous length. To make a flat welting, fold the bias strip in half, right sides out and long edges matching. On the right side of the textile panel, pin the flat welting, beginning at the center of 1 side of the panel and aligning its raw edges with those of the panel (see Figure 2). Clip the welting's seam allowance at the corners. Where the welting ends meet, overlap them 1". On 1 end, turn under ½" and refold the fabric, concealing the raw ends of the welting strip. Using a ½" seam allowance and a long stitch length, baste the welting to the center textile. Pivot the stitching at the corners.

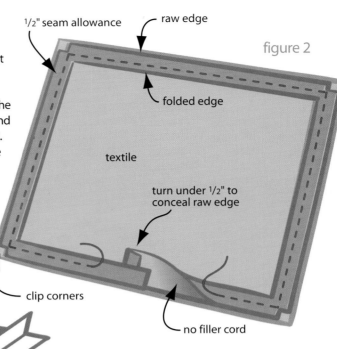

figure 2

½" seam allowance

raw edge

folded edge

textile

turn under ½" to conceal raw edge

clip corners

no filler cord

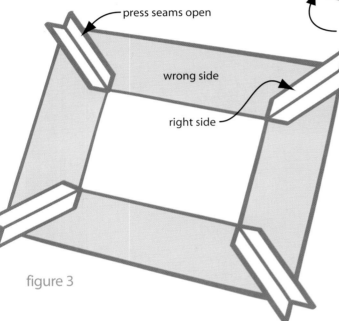

press seams open

wrong side

right side

figure 3

6 With right sides together and raw edges aligned, pin the border strips together at the corners on the angled edges. Using a ½" seam allowance, stitch each corner seam and press each seam open (see Figure 3).

7 With right sides together and raw edges aligned, pin the textile panel to the border. Remove a few stitches in the miter seams, if necessary, to fit the border to the panel. Using a ½" seam allowance, stitch the borders to the center panel along the previous basting line for the flat welting in the textile panel. Pivot the stitching at the corners. Grade the seam allowances and press the seam open. Turn to the right side and press the seam (see Figure 4).

8 Lay the front panel and the back panel right side up, matching bottom edges. Place the zipper between the panels. Follow the manufacturer's instructions to install the zipper between the panels.

9 With right sides together and raw edges aligned, pin the front panel to the back panel on the side edges (those adjacent to the zipper edge). Using a ½" seam allowance, stitch the panels together. Press the seam.

10 Open the zipper. With right sides together, place the side seams on the edges and align the top raw edges of the front panel and back panel. Pin. Align the raw edges of the bottom edges on each end of the zipper in the same manner. Pin. On the top edge, use a ½" seam allowance to stitch the edges together. Using a zipper foot, stitch the ends of the seam on the bottom edge in the same manner. Press the seams open. Turn to the right side through the zipper and insert the pillow form.

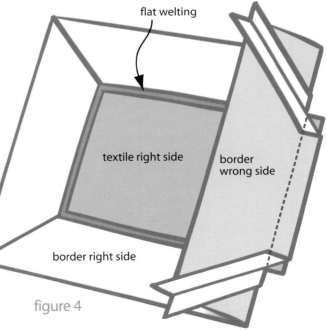

flat welting

textile right side

border wrong side

border right side

figure 4

For a tailored edging that gives a plain pillow more impact, add a flange. The flange design is simply an extended knife-edge pillow, with a pocket at the center to hold the pillow form. The contrast between the flat flange and the plump pillow makes the cushion look more generous and comfortable.

flange
pillow

The extended frame around the flange pillow enhances its decorative impact in the room by creating a larger splash of color and pattern. The flat border is usually 2 to 4 inches wide, but you may want to make the flange larger or smaller, depending on the size of the pillow and the fabric's motif. A small accent pillow made from a tiny print, for example, could be framed with an oversize flange to give it more importance, or with a narrow one to emphasize its petite dimensions.

Take cues from your fabric, too, for the width of the flange. Use checks and plaids as units to determine the width of the border. If you're working with a floral design, consider the best frame for the largest blossom or bouquet in the fabric. The instructions on the pages that follow make a pillow that measures 30 inches square overall, with a 3-inch-wide flange surrounding a 24-inch-square pillow form.

materials

24"-square pillow form
2 yards 54"-wide decorator
   fabric
1 yard 54"-wide contrast
   decorator fabric
4 yards $^6/_{32}$" filler cord

sewing tools

Sewing machine
Iron and ironing board
Fabric marking pen or pencil
Pins
Needles
Thread
Scissors
Tape measure
Liquid ravel preventer

skill level: beginner
time required: 2½ hours

flange pillow:

1 From the main decorator fabric, cut 2 (31") squares for the front and back panels. On geometric fabrics and florals, center motifs on the squares to achieve a balanced or symmetrical placement.

2 From contrast fabric, cut 4 yards of 1½"-wide bias strips. Stitch the strips together at the short ends to make a continuous length. To make welting, fold the bias strip around the cord, with wrong sides together and long raw edges matching. Using a zipper foot and a long stitch length, baste close to the cord, encasing the cord in the fabric cover.

3 Beginning at the center of the bottom edge of the panel, pin the welting to the right side of the front panel, with raw edges aligned. Clip the seam allowance of the welting at the corners. Where the welting ends meet, overlap the ends 1". Remove the stitching from the fabric cover on each end. Unfold the fabric and cut the ends of the cord to meet. Refold 1 end of the cover over the cord. On the remaining end, turn the cover under ½" and refold the fabric around the cord. Using a zipper foot and a long stitch length, baste the welting to the front panel (see Figure 1).

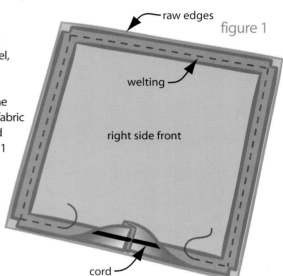

raw edges

figure 1

welting

right side front

cord

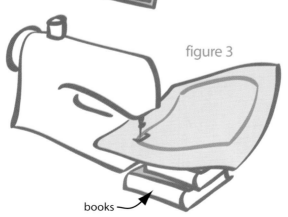

welting

figure 2

2"

2"

2"

2"

2"

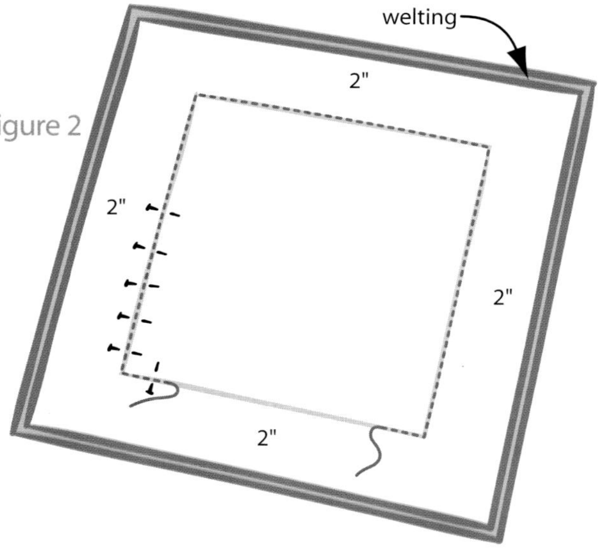

4 With right sides together and raw edges aligned, stitch the front panel to the back panel, using a zipper foot and following the basting line on the front panel. Stitch all corners, pivoting the stitching at the corners and leaving a long opening in the bottom edge for turning. Clip the corners and grade the seam allowances. Press the seam, then turn to the right side. Place the seam on the edge and press flat.

5 Measure and mark a line 2" from each edge of the pillow (see Figure 2). Pin the layers together along the line. Topstitch on the line, stitching all corners and pivoting the stitching at the corners. Leave an opening in the bottom (aligned with the opening in the outer bottom edge) to insert the pillow form.

6 Insert the pillow form into the cover. Shake the pillow away from the bottom edge and openings. Pin the front and back layers together along the marked line at the bottom of the pillow form. Topstitch along the line (see Figure 3). It is helpful to have someone support the pillow as you topstitch this edge of the pocket closed. If you are working alone, stack books beside the sewing machine to support the pillow. Hand-stitch the opening at the welt edge closed. Fluff the pillow to distribute the filling in the center pocket.

figure 3

books

MORE GOOD IDEAS

low-sew option

Instead of basting a pocket at the center of the pillow cover, use buttons to outline the pillow form. Mark points for 16 buttons around the area to be filled by the pillow. Stitch the buttons to the cover through both the top and back panels of the cover. For a fully finished look, tack a second group of 16 buttons over the threads on the back panel.

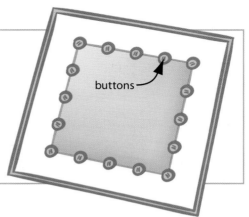

buttons

VARIATIONS ON A THEME

creating a shaped flange:

Exercise your creativity with custom-shaped edges that make the look unique to your home. Outline the wavy edge with welting for emphasis and definition.

1 Determine the finished size of the pillow at its widest and tallest point and add 1" to the side-to-side measure and to the top-to-bottom measure. From fabric, cut the front and back panels to this size. Set the back panel aside.

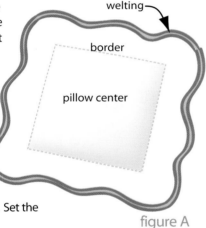

welting

border

pillow center

figure A

2 On the right side of the top panel, measure and mark lines 1/2" from each raw edge. Measure the finished width of the flange from this line toward the panel center. Mark a line here to show the stitching line for the pillow center.

3 Make a paper pattern of the shape you desire for the pillow edge. Place this pattern along each edge and trace the stitching line (see Figure B).

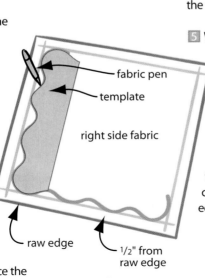

fabric pen

template

right side fabric

raw edge

1/2" from raw edge

figure B

Do not allow the stitching line to intrude on the 1/2" allowance at the raw edges.

4 Pin and baste welting to the right side of the top panel. Place the basting line in the welting along the marked stitching line of the shaped edge on the top panel (see Figure C). Clip the seam allowance of the welting as needed to ease the welting around the curves. Finish the ends of the welting. Trim the top panel to meet the raw edges of the welting.

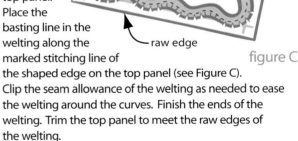

marked line

right side

raw edge

figure C

5 With right sides together, center the top panel on the bottom panel. Pin the layers together along the basting line for the welting, then stitch the panels together along the basting line. Stitch around all corners, leaving a long opening in one edge for turning. Trim the bottom panel even with the seam allowance of the top panel. Trim the edges of the opening even in the same manner. Clip the curves and turn the cover to the right side. Place the welting-trimmed seam on the edge and press flat. Finish the center pocket in the pillow as for the cover with straight edges, *Steps 5 and 6, opposite.*

Turn a bay window into a cozy seating nook

with a collection of pillows. Start with a box cushion for the window seat itself and add pillows in a variety of shapes and sizes. Details, such as the shirred edging on the seat cushion and button trim on the pillow, impart a designer look to basic shapes.

window seat collection

The shirred edging on the box cushion is called a ruche gusset—a gathered fabric that forms the box's sides. Such an edging adds rich texture to the cushion; it is a good technique for dressing up seat pads for dining chairs or for adding a touch of luxury to a cushion for a dressing-table bench. A zippered back gusset makes the covers easily removable when you need to have them dry-cleaned.

The cushion is cut from upholstery foam, which you can find in fabric stores. To cut the foam, use a serrated knife or an electric knife. Wrap the foam in batting for a smoother, plumper shape.

These pillows show the versatility of a few basic techniques. Combine one or more to create distinctive pillows for chairs, sofas, or benches. Buttons add charm to the rectangular pillow, which is defined top and bottom with piping and with fringe at the sides. Decorative loop fringe embellishes the double-flange pillow behind it, and brush fringe stitched into the seam outlines the floral-stripe pillows at the back.

materials

2"-thick high-density
   upholstery foam
Polyester fiberfill batting
Muslin
54"-wide decorator fabric
Zipper
Medium-weight nonwoven
   interfacing
Cording with lip
Dry-cleaning bag

tools

Electric knife or serrated knife

sewing tools

Sewing machine
Iron and ironing board
Fabric marking pen or pencil
Pins
Needles
Thread
Scissors
Tape measure
Liquid ravel preventer

skill level: advanced
time required: 9½ hours

ruche gusset box cushion:

1 Measure the window seat from front to back and from side to side (see Figure 1). For long spans, consider making 2 cushions for the space instead of 1 extra-long cushion. When using 2 cushions, subtract 1" from the side-to-side measurement for ease.

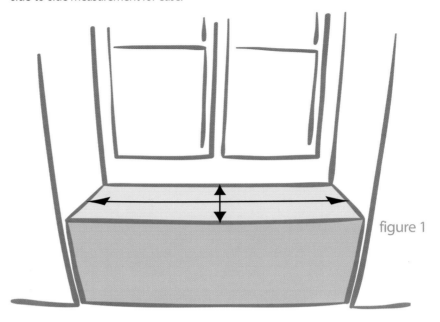

figure 1

2 Cut the foam to the window seat dimensions (less ½" to allow for the batting). Wrap it in batting, pinning and trimming the batting to cover the foam smoothly. Loosely sew the batting edges together by hand.

3 To make a muslin sleeve for the batting-wrapped cushion, measure the girth of the cushion and add 2". Measure the cushion from side to side, including the depth of both ends, and add 2". Cut 1 piece of muslin to this size. (Muslin is available in extra-wide widths so that you can cut this piece from a single length of fabric. If you must seam fabric to make up the required width, place the seam on a corner of the cushion.)

4 Center the muslin over the cushion and smooth the fabric around it, wrapping tightly. Turn under the raw edges on one long side. Align these edges with a corner of the cushion. Using a needle and thread, make tiny stitches by hand to secure (see Figure 2). Fold each end of the muslin cover as if wrapping a package, minimizing as much bulk as possible. Stitch by hand to secure the folded edges.

muslin

foam

figure 2

5 Measure the cushion top from side to side and front to back. Add 1" to each measurement. From the fabric, cut 2 pieces to this size for the top and bottom panels. If working with stripes or plaids, place them symmetrically on each panel and center any floral motifs or other prominent patterns. To determine the best placement of the fabric design, drape the cushion with the fabric before you cut.

6 Measure the back edge of the cushion and add 9". From the fabric, cut 2 (4"-wide) strips to this length, matching the pattern across the long edges for the zippered back gusset. With right sides together, long raw edges aligned, and patterns matching, baste the strips together on one long edge, using a $3/4$" seam allowance. Press the seam open. On the wrong side, center the zipper facedown or tab side down over the basted seam (see Figure 3). Using a needle and thread, baste the zipper tapes to the fabric by hand. Turn to the right side. Using a zipper foot, stitch the zipper in place following the manufacturer's instructions for centered zipper installation. Remove all basting stitches. Trim the strip to $3^1/2$" wide with the zipper at the center.

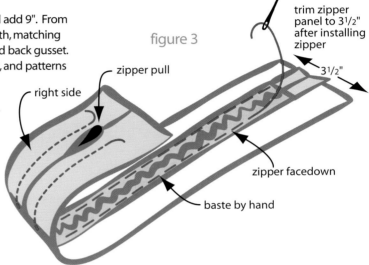

figure 3

trim zipper panel to $3^1/2$" after installing zipper

$3^1/2$"

zipper pull

right side

zipper facedown

baste by hand

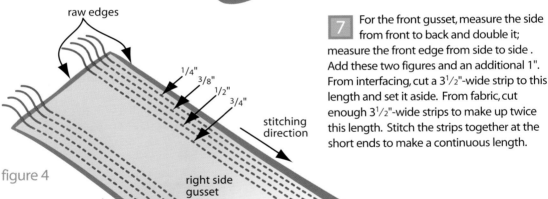

figure 4

raw edges

$1/4$"
$3/8$"
$1/2$"
$3/4$"

stitching direction

right side gusset

stitching direction

7 For the front gusset, measure the side from front to back and double it; measure the front edge from side to side . Add these two figures and an additional 1". From interfacing, cut a $3^1/2$"-wide strip to this length and set it aside. From fabric, cut enough $3^1/2$"-wide strips to make up twice this length. Stitch the strips together at the short ends to make a continuous length.

8 Set the sewing machine for a long stitch length and loosen the upper thread tension. Working from the right side of the long fabric strip for the gusset, sew 4 lines of gathering stitches on each long side $3/4$", $1/2$", $3/8$", and $1/4$" from the raw edge (see Figure 4). To create even gathers in the ruche, sew all lines of gathering stitches in the same direction. (Do not sew down 1 side and flip the strip around, sewing up the second side, as this will cause uneven gathering.)

ruche gusset box cushion continued

9 To gather the fabric, pull up the bobbin thread of all 4 stitching lines together on each side of gusset. Fit the gathered fabric to the length of interfacing strip. Adjust the gathers evenly along the length. Using both hands, tug each side of the gathered strip to straighten the gathers across the width of the piece. Pin the gathered fabric to the interfacing. Firmly press the gathers along the stitching lines. Lightly press the gathers between the stitching lines to set the folds.

10 Using a normal stitch length and thread tension, stitch the fabric to the interfacing on each edge following the gathering line $1/2$" from edge (see Figure 5). Stitch each edge in the same direction as before.

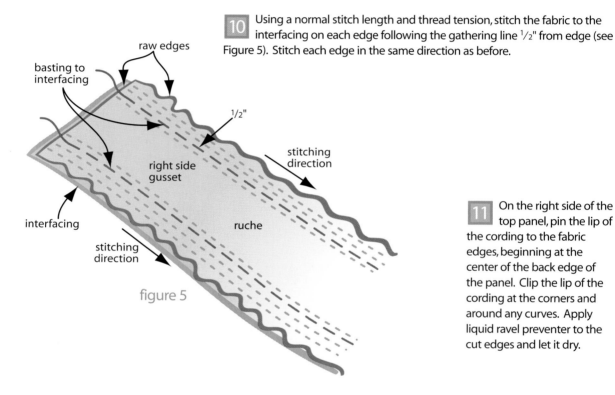

raw edges

basting to interfacing

$1/2$"

right side gusset

stitching direction

interfacing

ruche

stitching direction

figure 5

11 On the right side of the top panel, pin the lip of the cording to the fabric edges, beginning at the center of the back edge of the panel. Clip the lip of the cording at the corners and around any curves. Apply liquid ravel preventer to the cut edges and let it dry.

12 Where the cording meets, overlap the ends 2". Carefully remove the stitches that hold the cord to the lip for 1" to $1/4$" on each end (see Figure 6).

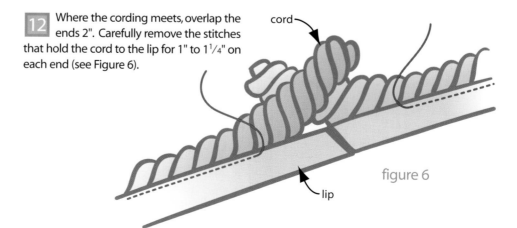

cord

lip

figure 6

13 At one end, gently unwrap the cords. Apply liquid ravel preventer to the ends of each cord in the trim. Let dry. Turn the raveled cord across the lip, keeping the tension on the twists to maintain the look of twisted cord. Using a needle and thread, stitch the raveled ends of the cord to the lip by hand (see Figure 7). Repeat at the opposite end of the cord.

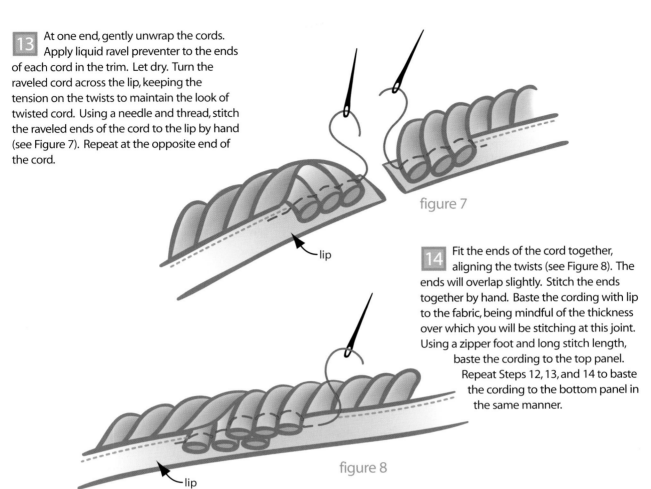

figure 7

lip

14 Fit the ends of the cord together, aligning the twists (see Figure 8). The ends will overlap slightly. Stitch the ends together by hand. Baste the cording with lip to the fabric, being mindful of the thickness over which you will be stitching at this joint. Using a zipper foot and long stitch length, baste the cording to the top panel. Repeat Steps 12, 13, and 14 to baste the cording to the bottom panel in the same manner.

figure 8

lip

15 With right sides together and raw edges aligned, center the zippered gusset back on the back edge of the bottom panel (see Figure 9). Position the pins on the wrong side of the gusset to sew the seam from that side of the fabric. Using a zipper foot and a long stitch length, baste the back gusset to the long back edge, starting and stopping the seam at each corner. Do not sew around the corner. Clip the seam allowances of the back gusset to each corner.

16 With right sides together and raw edges aligned, center the front gusset on the front edge of the bottom panel. Position the pins on the wrong side of the gusset to sew the seam from that side of the fabric. Using a zipper foot and a long stitch length, baste the front gusset to the long front edge, starting and stopping the seam at each corner. Do not sew around the corner. Clip the seam allowance of the front gusset to each corner.

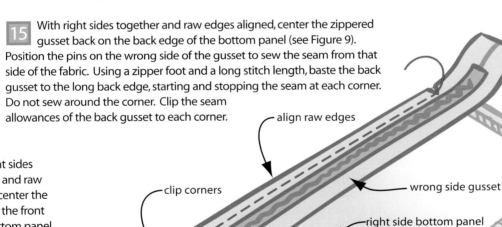

align raw edges

clip corners

wrong side gusset

right side bottom panel

cording

figure 9

ruche gusset box cushion continued

17 With right sides together and raw edges aligned, pin the back gusset (where the zipper stop is located) and front gusset to the side edge of the bottom panel (see Figure 10). Bring the short ends of the gussets together, with right sides facing, to the seam line of the gusset back and gusset front. Stitch the back gusset and front gusset together at the bottom of the zipper. (The seam allowances will be of differing depths on the front and back gussets.) Trim the seam allowance to $\frac{1}{2}$". Trim the interfacing in the seam allowance from the front gusset and press the seam toward the front gusset. Repin the gusset to the bottom panel on that side. Position the pins on the wrong side of the gusset to sew the seam from that side of the fabrics. Using a zipper foot and long stitch length, baste the gusset to the side edge of the bottom panel, stitching around the corners. Pivot the stitching at the corners.

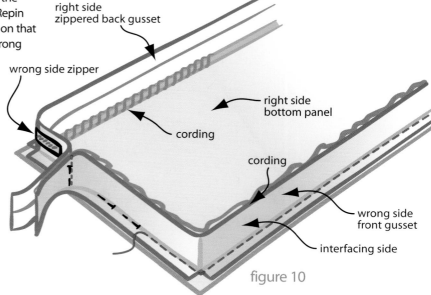

right side
zippered back gusset

wrong side zipper

right side
bottom panel

cording

cording

wrong side
front gusset

interfacing side

figure 10

18 With right sides together and raw edges aligned, pin the back gusset and front gusset to the remaining side edge of the bottom panel. Bring the short ends of the gussets together, with right sides facing. Make a 1"-deep tuck at the end of the gusset front to cover the zipper tab (see Figure 11). Trim the end of the front gusset to match the back gusset. Stitch the back gusset and front gusset together at the top of the zipper. Trim the interfacing from the back of the front gusset in the seam allowance. Press the seam toward the front gusset. Repin the gusset to the bottom panel. Position the pins on the wrong side of the top panel to sew the seam from that side of the fabrics. Using the zipper foot and a long stitch length, baste the gusset to the side edge of the bottom panel, stitching around the corners. Pivot the stitching at the corners.

figure 11

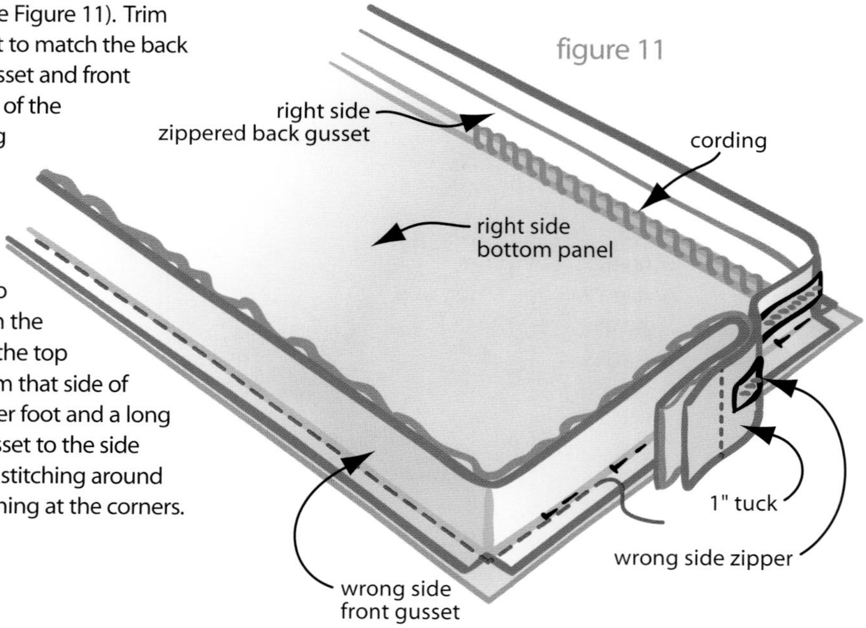

right side
zippered back gusset

cording

right side
bottom panel

1" tuck

wrong side zipper

wrong side
front gusset

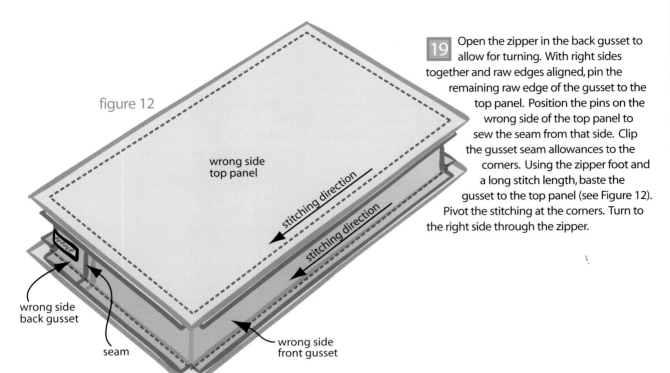

figure 12

wrong side
top panel

stitching direction

stitching direction

wrong side
back gusset

seam

wrong side
front gusset

19 Open the zipper in the back gusset to allow for turning. With right sides together and raw edges aligned, pin the remaining raw edge of the gusset to the top panel. Position the pins on the wrong side of the top panel to sew the seam from that side. Clip the gusset seam allowances to the corners. Using the zipper foot and a long stitch length, baste the gusset to the top panel (see Figure 12). Pivot the stitching at the corners. Turn to the right side through the zipper.

20 Look at the right side of each seam. The fabrics should fit together smoothly without puckers. Remove stitches if necessary and restitch to make each seam smooth. Return the stitch length to the normal setting. Turn the cushion cover to the wrong side again and sew the gusset to the top panel along the basting lines, working with the wrong side of the top panel facing you (see Figure 13). Sew the gusset to the bottom panel along the basting lines, working with the wrong side of the gusset facing you. Remove the gathering stitches from the right side of the gusset by pulling the bobbin thread and then the upper thread. Tear or trim the interfacing from the wrong side of the gusset and seam allowances. Press the seams.

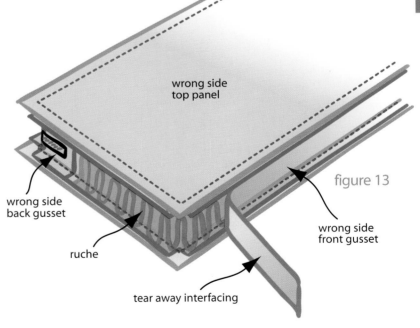

wrong side
top panel

wrong side
back gusset

ruche

figure 13

wrong side
front gusset

tear away interfacing

21 Turn the cover to the right side. Wrap the cushion in plastic. Insert the cushion in the cover through the opening. Adjust the cushion to match the top and bottom corners at the cording. Remove the plastic. Close the zipper.

materials

14"-square feather/down
   pillow form
1 yard 54"-wide decorator
   fabric
2 yards decorative loop fringe

sewing tools

Sewing machine
Iron and ironing board
Fabric marking pen and
   pencil
Pins
Needles
Thread
Invisible thread
Scissors
Tape measure
Liquid ravel preventer

skill level: intermediate
time required: 4 hours

pillow with double flange:

1 From paper, cut a 6" square to make a template for mitered corners. Fold the paper once from corner to corner. Crease the fold. Mark an X on the corner that is not folded. Cut the paper square into 2 triangles by cutting along the crease. Discard one triangle. Mark the paper triangle "Template." Note: The corner of the triangle marked with an X is a 90-degree angle.

2 From fabric, cut 2 (24") squares for the front and back panels. Center any prominent fabric motifs or symmetrically place geometric designs.

3 Place the template on a corner of the front panel (see Figure 1). Fit the 90-degree corner of the template into the corner of the panel. Align the sides of the template with the raw edges of the panel. Using a fabric marker, make a line on the panel along the long side of the template. Mark the remaining corners of the front panel and all corners of the back panel in the same manner.

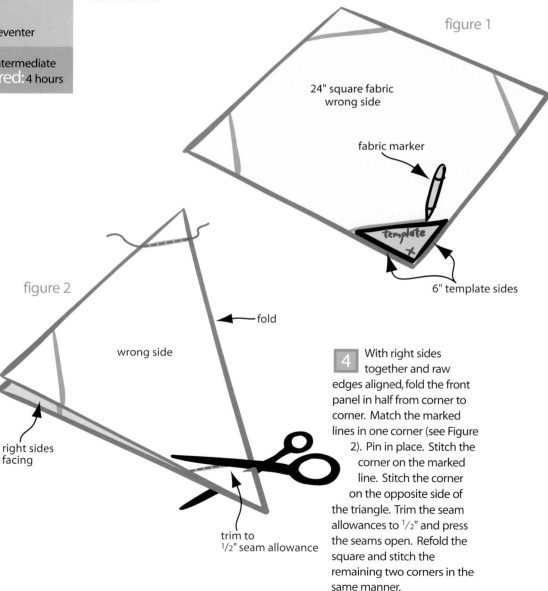

figure 1

24" square fabric
wrong side

fabric marker

template

6" template sides

figure 2

fold

wrong side

right sides
facing

trim to
1/2" seam allowance

4 With right sides together and raw edges aligned, fold the front panel in half from corner to corner. Match the marked lines in one corner (see Figure 2). Pin in place. Stitch the corner on the marked line. Stitch the corner on the opposite side of the triangle. Trim the seam allowances to 1/2" and press the seams open. Refold the square and stitch the remaining two corners in the same manner.

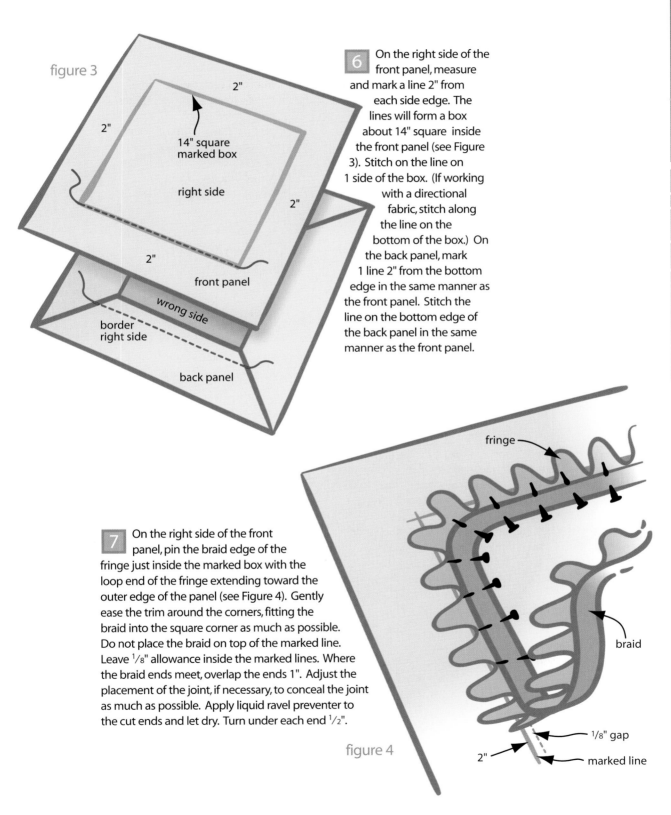

5 On each panel, turn the stitched corners to the wrong side of the panel, forming a mitered turn. Press.

figure 3

2"

2"

14" square marked box

right side

2"

2"

front panel

wrong side

border right side

back panel

6 On the right side of the front panel, measure and mark a line 2" from each side edge. The lines will form a box about 14" square inside the front panel (see Figure 3). Stitch on the line on 1 side of the box. (If working with a directional fabric, stitch along the line on the bottom of the box.) On the back panel, mark 1 line 2" from the bottom edge in the same manner as the front panel. Stitch the line on the bottom edge of the back panel in the same manner as the front panel.

7 On the right side of the front panel, pin the braid edge of the fringe just inside the marked box with the loop end of the fringe extending toward the outer edge of the panel (see Figure 4). Gently ease the trim around the corners, fitting the braid into the square corner as much as possible. Do not place the braid on top of the marked line. Leave 1/8" allowance inside the marked lines. Where the braid ends meet, overlap the ends 1". Adjust the placement of the joint, if necessary, to conceal the joint as much as possible. Apply liquid ravel preventer to the cut ends and let dry. Turn under each end 1/2".

figure 4

fringe

braid

1/8" gap

2"

marked line

8 Thread the machine with invisible thread on top and conventional thread in the bobbin. Using a normal stitch length, stitch the braid to the front panel following the edge of the braid next to the fringe. Pivot the stitching at the corners. Working in the same direction, stitch the remaining edge of the braid to the front panel, easing the braid into the corners. To keep control of the stitches in the corners, you may need to shorten the stitch length. (When the machine makes more stitches per inch, you have greater control of the placement of each stitch.)

9 With wrong sides together and turned edges aligned, stack the front panel on the back panel (see Figure 5). Match the stitched lines from Step 6 along the bottom edge of each panel. These stitched lines will be at the opening in the bottom of the pillow cover where you insert the pillow form. Lift the fringe to reveal the marked line on the front panel and pin the panels together along the marked line.

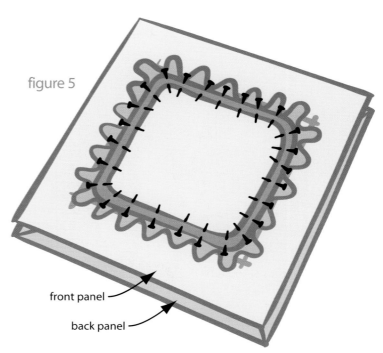

figure 5

front panel

back panel

10 Using a zipper foot and beginning 1" from the corner and following the line of stitches on the bottom edge of the marked box, stitch to the corner. Keep the fringe free. Pivot the stitching. Stitch the remaining sides to make a pocket for the pillow form. Pivot the stitching at the corners. Stop stitching 1" into the line of stitches on the bottom edge. Leave the center section of the bottom edge of the pocket open.

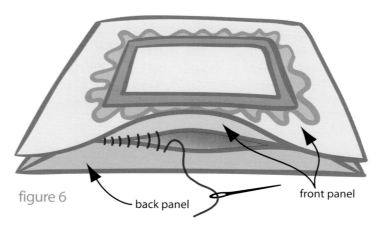

figure 6

back panel

front panel

11 Insert the pillow form into the pocket through the opening. Using a needle and thread, make small stitches by hand between the front panel and back panel along the lines of stitches to close the opening (see Figure 6).

double flange with contrast facing:

Create interest by facing the edges of the panels in the double flange pillow with a boldly contrasting fabric. To make the contrast facing, follow these instructions; they will make a cover for a 14"-square pillow.

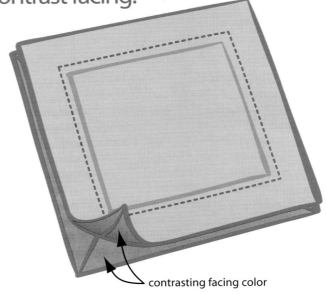

contrasting facing color

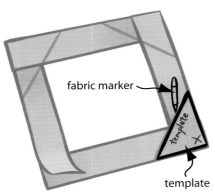

fabric marker

template

figure A

1 Make the template as described in Step 1, page 42.

2 From fabric, cut 2 (19") squares for the front and back panels. From contrast fabric, cut 8 facing strips 3"×24".

3 Lay out 4 facing strips wrong side up. Set the remaining strips aside. With raw edges aligned, stack 1 end of 2 adjacent strips to form the corner. Place the template made in Step 1 on the corner of the stack. The long edge of the template will cross the inside corner of the facings (see Figure A). Mark the stitching line on the facings by tracing along the long edge of the template. Mark 1 pair of facing strips at a time. Repeat for the remaining 4 facing strips.

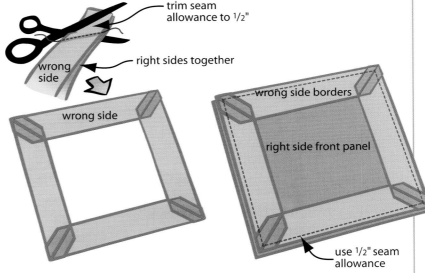

trim seam allowance to 1/2"

right sides together

wrong side

wrong side

figure B

wrong side borders

right side front panel

use 1/2" seam allowance

figure C

4 With right sides together, raw edges aligned, and matching marked lines, stitch the facings on the marked line. Trim the seam allowance to 1/2" (see Figure B). Press the seam open. Mark and stitch the remaining facing strips in the same manner.

5 With right sides together and raw edges aligned, pin the front panel to one facing square. Using a 1/2" seam allowance, stitch each edge. Pivot

the stitching at the corners. Clip the corners and press the seam open (see Figure C).

6 Turn the facing to the wrong side, placing the seam on the edge. Press flat. Follow the instructions from Step 9, page 44 (disregarding reference to fringe).

button-front pillow:

1 From fabric cut 1 (18"×15") back panel, 1 (16"×15") front panel, and 1 (6"×15") side front panel. Cut 2 yards of 1$^1/_2$"-wide bias strips. Stitch the strips together at the short ends to make a continuous length.

2 To make welting, fold the bias strip around the cord, matching the long raw edges. Using a zipper foot and a long stitch length, baste close to the cord, encasing the cord in the fabric cover. Set the welting aside.

3 On the front panel, turn under 2" along one 15" edge. Press. Cover the buttons with scraps of complementary fabric, following the manufacturer's instructions. Evenly space the buttons on the front of the panel along the turned edge (see Figure 1). With the right side of the fabric faceup, lap the button-trimmed edge of the front panel over the side front panel. Position the panels to make an 18"×15" panel. Using a long stitch length, baste the lapped panels along the raw edges.

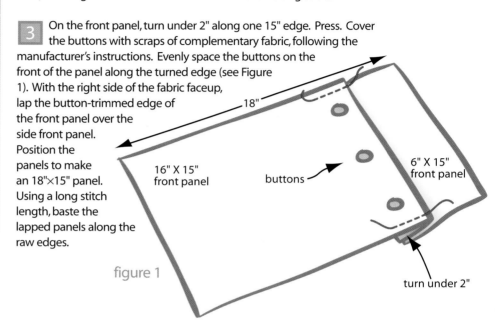

18"
16" X 15" front panel
buttons
6" X 15" front panel
turn under 2"

figure 1

4 On the right side of the front panel, place the braid edge of the fringe inside the $^1/_2$" seam allowance so the tassel fringe extends over the raw edges of the panel. Thread the machine with invisible thread in the top and conventional thread in the bobbin. Using a long stitch length, topstitch the braid portion of the fringe to the front panel on each short edge. Stitch each edge of the braid in the same direction. This will prevent puckering in the finished front panel. (Do not stitch down one edge and up the other; this will cause puckering.) Turn the panel to the wrong side and press the stitching.

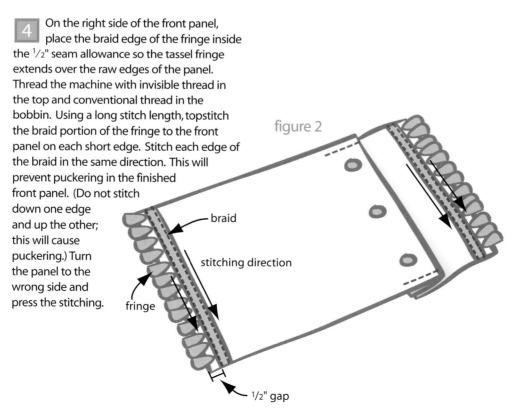

figure 2

braid
stitching direction
fringe
$^1/_2$" gap

5 On the right side of the front panel, pin the welting, aligning raw edges (see Figure 3). Begin at the center of the side edge to conceal the joint in the welting under the tassel fringe. (Keep the fringe out of the seam.) Overlap the raw ends of the braid at each end with the welting. Clip the welting seam allowance at the corners. Where the welting ends meet, overlap the ends 1". Remove the stitching from the fabric cover on each end. Unfold the fabric and cut the ends of cord to meet. Refold 1 end of the cover over the cord. On the remaining end, turn the cover under $1/2$" and refold the fabric around the cord, concealing the raw ends of the fabric cover. Using a zipper foot and a long stitch length, baste the welting to the front panel. Pivot the stitching at the corners.

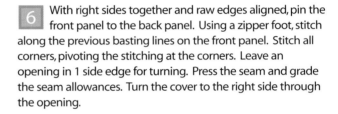

folded edge
cord
turn under $1/2$"
figure 3
welting

6 With right sides together and raw edges aligned, pin the front panel to the back panel. Using a zipper foot, stitch along the previous basting lines on the front panel. Stitch all corners, pivoting the stitching at the corners. Leave an opening in 1 side edge for turning. Press the seam and grade the seam allowances. Turn the cover to the right side through the opening.

7 Insert the pillow form into the cover through the opening. Turn the raw edges along the opening to the inside of the pillow. Using a needle and thread, stitch the opening closed by hand.

add personality with buttons

Buttons lend a high-style, fashion-influenced look to pillows and other home decorating projects. You can find buttons for every taste and style. Fabric-covered buttons suggest a traditional decorating scheme. Bakelite buttons found at your favorite flea market are perfect accessories for retro-style homes. Sophisticated shell buttons, such as mother-of-pearl and abalone, suit an elegant setting.

Collecting vintage buttons is a fast-growing hobby. Antiques stores, flea markets, and specialty button shops offer a treasure of these useful and beautiful gems.

For handmade interest, look for clay and polymer pieces sold by artists at large crafts shows. Many of these are miniature works of art. Use them on a pillow and you'll have a new and interesting conversation piece.

Ruffled pillows create country charm and add comfort to ordinary dining chairs. For a well-coordinated look, use a large-scale print for the tablecloth and window treatment and cut out one motif from the print to frame a pillow made from coordinating fabric. Piping or welting outlines the motif and gives the pillow front dimension and texture.

gathered & pleated ruffles

This pillow design works equally well for a country-style family room or bedroom. In these settings, the large-scale floral that supplies the center motif might slipcover the sofa or dress the bed.

When you create a ruffled pillow collection, keep the proportion of the pillow body to the ruffle in mind. If the ruffle is too wide, it will lose body, flop, and overwhelm the design. If the ruffle is too narrow, it will look unfinished. In the chair *at left*, the large (18-inch) blue and white pillow has an appropriately scaled ruffle that is 3 inches wide.

The width of the ruffle balances the center panel of the pillow body, which shows off a large floral motif. Each component—the motif on the center panel and the ruffle—has equal importance, creating a balance that pleases the eye. On the smaller pillow, a narrow, pleated ruffle complements the diminutive scale of the floral.

materials

18"-square pillow form
Tracing or tissue paper
3/4 yard 54"-wide decorator
    fabric (check)
1 3/4 yards 54"-wide accent
    decorator fabric (floral)
4 yards 6/32" filler cord
16" zipper

sewing tools

Sewing machine
Iron and ironing board
Fabric marking pen or pencil
Pins
Needles
Thread
Scissors
Tape measure
Liquid ravel preventer

skill level: advanced
time required: 7 hours

gathered ruffles:

1 From fabric, cut 2 (19") squares for the front panel and back panel. Cut 1 (2"×19") zipper panel. If you are working with a fabric that has a prominent motif or design, match the pattern from the back panel to the zipper panel. Set the panels aside.

2 From paper, cut 1 (13 1/2") square for the center panel pattern. Fold the paper in half from corner to corner and crease to mark the center. Open the fold and place the pattern on the accent fabric, aligning the center crease with the straight grain of the fabric. Center any prominent motif in the fabric under the pattern. Using the pattern as a guide, cut 1 center panel.

3 From the accent fabric, cut enough 7"-wide bias strips to make 4 yards for the ruffle. Stitch the strips together at the short ends to make a continuous length, then stitch the ends of the ruffle strip together to make a loop. With the wrong sides together and raw edges aligned, fold the ruffle in half. Press the fold to crease. Set aside.

4 From the accent fabric, cut enough 1 1/2"-wide bias strips to make 4 yards for the welting. Stitch the strips together at the short ends to make a continuous length. To make the welting, fold the bias strip around the cord, matching the long raw edges. Using a zipper foot and a long stitch length, baste close to the cord, encasing the cord in the fabric cover.

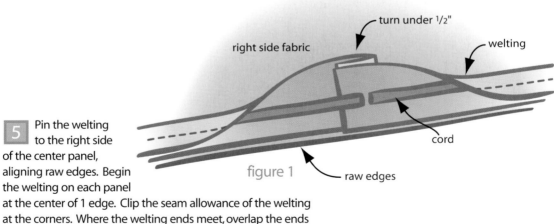

turn under 1/2"

welting

right side fabric

cord

figure 1

raw edges

5 Pin the welting to the right side of the center panel, aligning raw edges. Begin the welting on each panel at the center of 1 edge. Clip the seam allowance of the welting at the corners. Where the welting ends meet, overlap the ends 1". Remove the basting from the fabric cover on each end (see Figure 1). Unfold the fabric and cut the cord ends to meet. Refold 1 end of the cover over the cord. On the remaining end, turn the cover under 1/2" and refold the fabric around the cord, concealing the raw ends of the fabric cover. Using a zipper foot and long stitch length, baste the welting to the front panel. Pivot the stitching at the corners.

6. Apply the welting to the right side of the front panel in the same manner. At the corners, make a small curve instead of a sharp turn (see Figure 2). Make several clips in the seam allowance of the welting around the curve. This small curve will improve the look of the finished ruffled pillow.

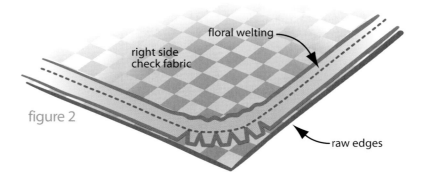

floral welting

right side
check fabric

figure 2

raw edges

7. On the center panel, turn under the raw edges of the panel and welting. Press. Stack the center panel on the right side of the front panel (see Figure 3). Position the center panel on point. Pin in place. Using a zipper foot, stitch in the ditch to topstitch the center panel to the front panel.

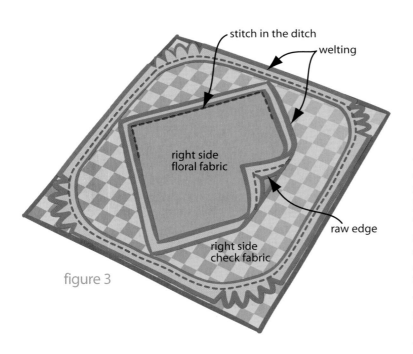

stitch in the ditch

welting

right side
floral fabric

raw edge

right side
check fabric

figure 3

8. Treating the long raw edges of the ruffle as 1, divide the ruffle into 4 quarters. Place pins at each quarter. Set the machine for a long stitch length and loosen the upper thread tension. Starting and stopping the stitching at each quarter mark, make 4 lines of gathering stitches $3/4$", $1/2$", $3/8$", and $1/4$" from the edge. To create even gathers in the ruffle, sew all lines of gathering stitches in the same direction and keep 1 side of the ruffle on top. Label the top side of the ruffle as the right side.

gathered ruffles continued

9 On the front panel, mark the center of each side with a pin to divide the edges of the panel into 4 quarters. Placing quarter marks at the center of the panel sides lets you fit the ruffle easily around the corners. With the right sides together and raw edges aligned, match the quarter marks on the ruffle to the quarter marks on the front panel (see Figure 4).

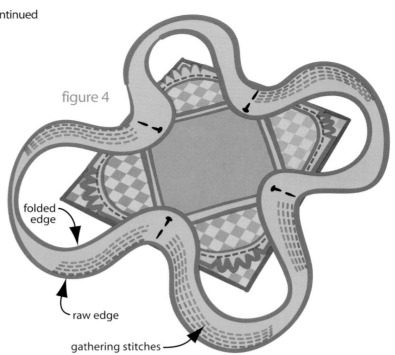

figure 4

folded edge

raw edge

gathering stitches

10 On the ruffle, pull up the bobbin thread of all 4 stitching lines together to fit the ruffle to the edge of the front panel. Adjust the gathers, placing them closer together around the corners. Using a zipper foot and long stitch length, baste the ruffle to the front panel along the basting line in the front panel, catching the welting in the stitches. Look at the right side of the ruffle to make sure the gathers are even. If necessary, remove the basting, adjust the gathers, and restitch. Press the seam allowance of the ruffle. From the wrong side of the front panel, press the seam.

11 Lay the back panel and the zipper panel right side up. The zipper is inserted between the back panel and the zipper panel. Center the zipper facedown on the top, long edge of the zipper panel (see Figure 5). Align the zipper tape with the raw edge of the panel. Using a zipper foot, stitch the zipper tape to the panel. Turn the zipper to the right side, turning the seam allowance under the panel. Press.

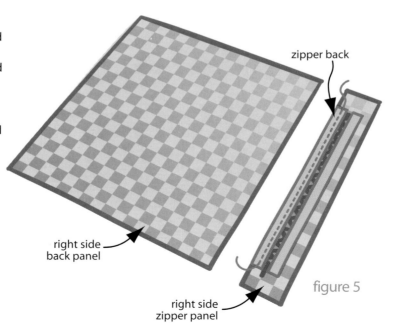

zipper back

right side back panel

right side zipper panel

figure 5

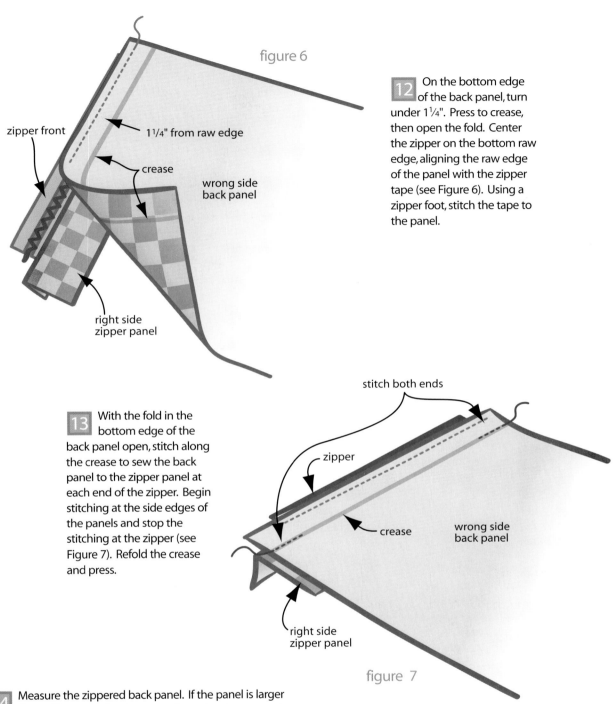

figure 6

zipper front

1¼" from raw edge

crease

wrong side
back panel

right side
zipper panel

12 On the bottom edge of the back panel, turn under 1¼". Press to crease, then open the fold. Center the zipper on the bottom raw edge, aligning the raw edge of the panel with the zipper tape (see Figure 6). Using a zipper foot, stitch the tape to the panel.

13 With the fold in the bottom edge of the back panel open, stitch along the crease to sew the back panel to the zipper panel at each end of the zipper. Begin stitching at the side edges of the panels and stop the stitching at the zipper (see Figure 7). Refold the crease and press.

stitch both ends

zipper

crease

wrong side
back panel

right side
zipper panel

figure 7

14 Measure the zippered back panel. If the panel is larger than 19" square, trim the excess from the zipper panel on the edge opposite the zipper. Open the zipper. With right sides together and raw edges aligned, stitch the back panel to the front panel along the previous basting in the front panel. Catch the welting and ruffle in the stitches. Clip the corners and grade the seam allowance. Press the seam.

15 Turn to the right side through the zipper and press the seams. To remove the visible lines of gathering stitches, pull the bobbin thread and then the top thread. Insert the pillow form into the cover through the zipper. Close the zipper.

pleated ruffles:

1 From fabric, cut 2 pieces 13"×17" for the front and back panels. Cut the panels to make the best display of the fabric design. Set the panels aside. From the accent fabric, on the straight grain of the fabric, cut enough 3"-wide strips to make 5 yards for the ruffle. With right sides together and raw edges aligned, stitch the strips together at the short ends, using a $1/4$" seam allowance and making a continuous length of 5 yards. Stitch the ends of the ruffle together to make a loop. Press the seams.

2 With wrong sides together and long raw edges matching, fold the ruffle in half and press. Treating both raw edges as 1, measure and mark $3/4$" segments (see Figure 1). Adjust the width of the segments as necessary to make the finished pleats appear even (slight adjustments will not be noticeable). Fold the ruffle at appropriate marks to form pleats. Pin to secure, then press lightly and remove the pins.

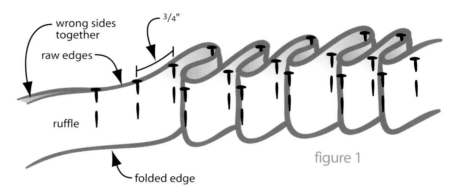

figure 1

3 Pin the ruffle to the right side of the front panel, aligning raw edges. Curve the edge of the ruffle around the corners (see Figure 2). In the finished pillow, the outer edge of the ruffle will spread like a fan around the corners. Using a $1/2$" seam allowance and a long stitch length, baste the ruffle to the front panel. Turn the ruffle out and check its appearance from the right side of the front panel. If necessary, remove the basting to adjust the pleats. Restitch, then press the seam allowance.

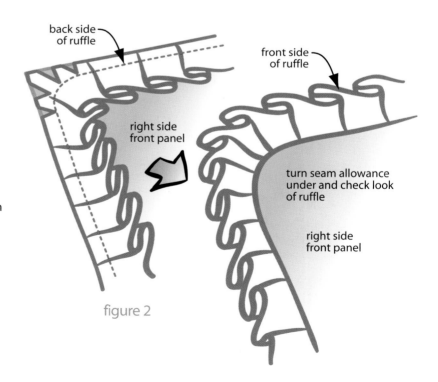

figure 2

4 Place the front and back panels with right sides facing up. Arrange the panels with the long, lower edges side by side. Center the zipper, right side or tab side up between the panels (see Figure 3). Follow the manufacturer's instructions to install the invisible zipper. Center the zipper tape on each fabric edge. Do not stitch the ends of the seam together at this time.

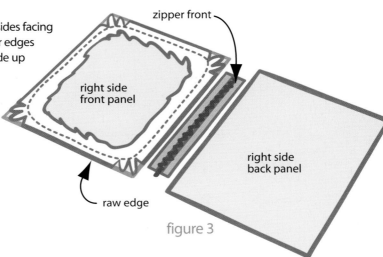

figure 3

5 With right sides together and raw edges aligned, pin the side edges of the back panel to the front panel. Using a ½" seam allowance, stitch the panels together on the pinned edges. Press the seam open. Turn to the right side. Press the seams.

6 Turn to the wrong side. With right sides together and raw edges aligned, pin the seams at each end of the zipper. Using a ½" seam allowance and zipper foot, stitch the ends of the seam. Press the seam open, then open the zipper. With right sides together and raw edges aligned, pin the remaining open edges of the pillow together. Using a ½" seam allowance, stitch the back panel to the front panel. Trim the corners, press the seam open, then turn to the right side through the zipper and press the seams.

7 Place the seams on the edge and straighten the pleats. Cover the pleats with a pressing cloth dampened with a vinegar and water solution. Press the pleats to make them permanent. Insert the pillow form through the zipper.

CUTTING RUFFLES ON THE BIAS

▪ How do you know when to cut a ruffle on the bias? The answer is easy. Think about the shape and form of the pillow that you would like to sew. Should the ruffle be soft and flowing, or should it be stiff and directed?

▪ Cutting on the bias takes advantage of the ability of a fabric to give or to stretch. To test this for yourself, cut a square piece of scrap fabric. Hold opposite sides of the square in your hands and pull firmly. Because you are pulling on the straight grain of the fabric, you won't feel much "give," but you'll notice how strong the fabric feels. Now, pull the fabric from opposite corners of the square, on the diagonal. You'll feel the stretch or give of the bias compared to the straight grain. When you want a ruffle that has a soft look, cut the ruffle strip on the bias. The blue floral pillow shown on page 48 has an unstructured ruffle that was sewn from a bias-cut strip of fabric.

▪ Fabric pieces cut on the straight grain are the most stable pieces. When you use a strip cut on the straight grain for a ruffle, you create a stiff or crisp ruffle. This is best for small pleated ruffles, which must maintain a crisp, sharp form in order to be attractive on the finished pillow.

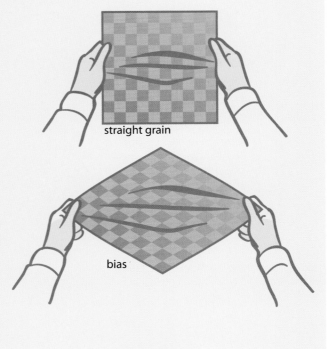

straight grain

bias

Look twice at the scalloped
ruffles on these throw pillows: The ruffle on each
pillow is constructed from half-round units stitched
into the seam between the front and back panels.
First gather each scalloped unit individually, somewhat
like a daisy petal, and then attach the gathered petals
to the pillow's edge.

scallop ruffle & variations

This ruffle treatment has more depth and complexity than an ordinary ruffle. It is especially suited to use in a bedroom where you want to create a setting that is comforting and soft, yet traditional in feeling.

To define the edges of the scallops without inserting cording or welting into each of the units, choose a coordinating fabric for the back of the pillow. In the room *opposite*, the scallops are backed with the same fabric used for the window treatment lining.

Because the pieced ruffle creates bulky seam allowances around the edges of the pillow, you will need to line the pillow front. This will help hide the construction, and if you are using a medium-weight to lightweight fabric, a lining will help stabilize it.

materials

16"-square pillow form
1 yard 54"-wide decorator
   fabric
1 yard 54"-wide coordinating
   decorator fabric
14" zipper
8"-diameter dessert or
   luncheon plate

sewing tools

Sewing machine
Iron and ironing board
Fabric marking pen or pencil
Seam ripper
Pins
Needles
Thread
Scissors
Tape measure
Iron and ironing board

skill level: advanced
time required: 9 hours

scallop ruffle:

1 From fabric, cut 1 (17") square for the front panel. From coordinating fabric, cut 2 (17") squares for the lining and back panel and 1 (2"×17") zipper panel.

2 With right sides together and raw edges aligned, stack the remaining fabric and coordinating fabric to cut shaped pieces for the border. Mark lines on the bias across the fabric every 6" (see Figure 1). These lines will help with placement of the half-round template.

3 With tape, mark off $^2/_3$ of a plate to make a template for the scallops. Place the plate facedown on the fabric, aligning the taped edge with a placement line on the fabric (see Figure 1). Trace along the edge of the plate. Repeat to mark 28 shaped units. Pin the layers of fabric together at the center of each marked unit to keep the layers together. Cut both layers as 1 on the marked lines. Keep the pieces pinned together.

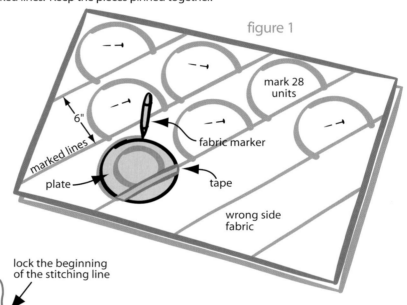

figure 1

mark 28 units

6"

marked lines

fabric marker

plate

tape

wrong side fabric

4 Using a $^1/_4$" seam allowance and a short stitch length (12 stitches per inch), stitch the raw edges of each unit along the curved edge. Press. Clip the seam allowance heavily, then press the seam. Turn to the right side and place the seam on the edge. Press flat.

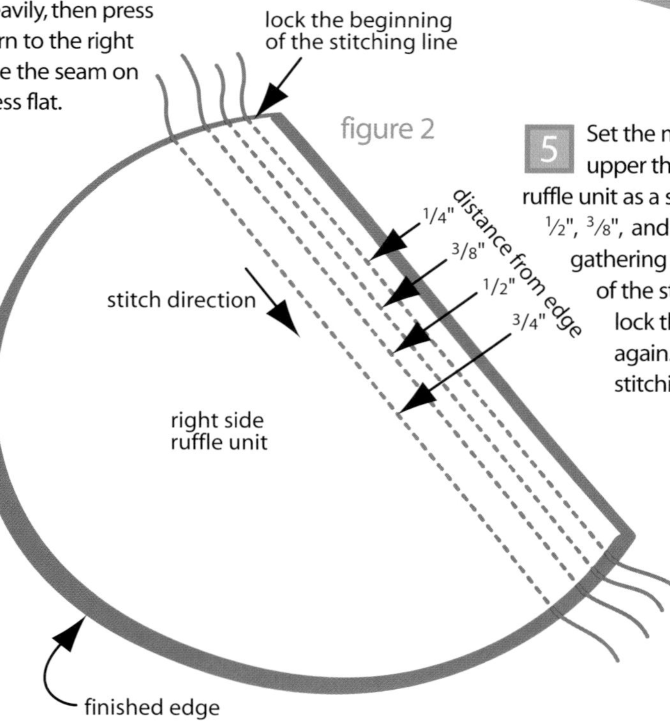

lock the beginning of the stitching line

figure 2

stitch direction

right side ruffle unit

distance from edge

$^1/_4$"
$^3/_8$"
$^1/_2$"
$^3/_4$"

finished edge

5 Set the machine for a long stitch length and loosen the upper thread tension. Treating the raw edges of each ruffle unit as a single layer, make lines of gathering stitches $^3/_4$", $^1/_2$", $^3/_8$", and $^1/_4$" from edge (see Figure 2). Stitch each line of gathering stitches in the same direction. At the beginning of the stitches, make 1 stitch, reverse the feed dog to lock the thread for 1 or 2 stitches, then stitch forward again. Do not lock the thread at the end of the stitching line. Leave long tails of thread.

6 Gather each ruffle unit to measure approximately $3^1/_2$" by pulling up the bobbin thread of all 4 stitching lines together. Knot the bobbin threads with the tails from the top threads to secure the gathers. Adjust the gathers along the edge so they're even.

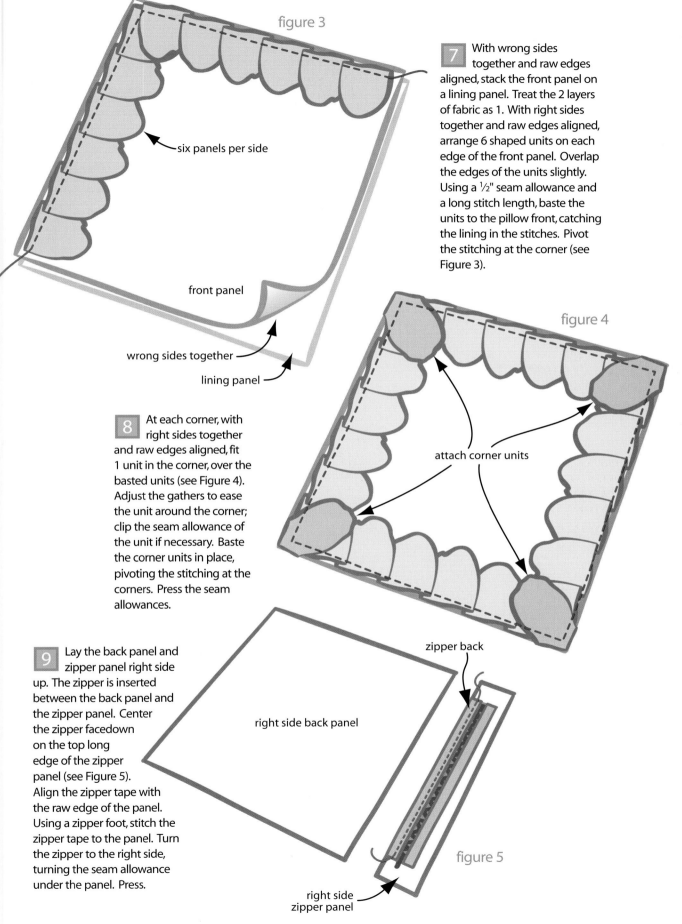

figure 3

six panels per side

front panel

wrong sides together

lining panel

7 With wrong sides together and raw edges aligned, stack the front panel on a lining panel. Treat the 2 layers of fabric as 1. With right sides together and raw edges aligned, arrange 6 shaped units on each edge of the front panel. Overlap the edges of the units slightly. Using a ½" seam allowance and a long stitch length, baste the units to the pillow front, catching the lining in the stitches. Pivot the stitching at the corner (see Figure 3).

figure 4

attach corner units

8 At each corner, with right sides together and raw edges aligned, fit 1 unit in the corner, over the basted units (see Figure 4). Adjust the gathers to ease the unit around the corner; clip the seam allowance of the unit if necessary. Baste the corner units in place, pivoting the stitching at the corners. Press the seam allowances.

9 Lay the back panel and zipper panel right side up. The zipper is inserted between the back panel and the zipper panel. Center the zipper facedown on the top long edge of the zipper panel (see Figure 5). Align the zipper tape with the raw edge of the panel. Using a zipper foot, stitch the zipper tape to the panel. Turn the zipper to the right side, turning the seam allowance under the panel. Press.

right side back panel

zipper back

figure 5

right side zipper panel

scallop ruffle continued

10 On the bottom edge of the back panel, turn under 1¼" and press to crease. Open the fold. Center the zipper on the bottom raw edge of the panel, aligning the raw edge of the panel with the zipper tape (see Figure 6). Using a zipper foot, stitch the tape to the panel. Press.

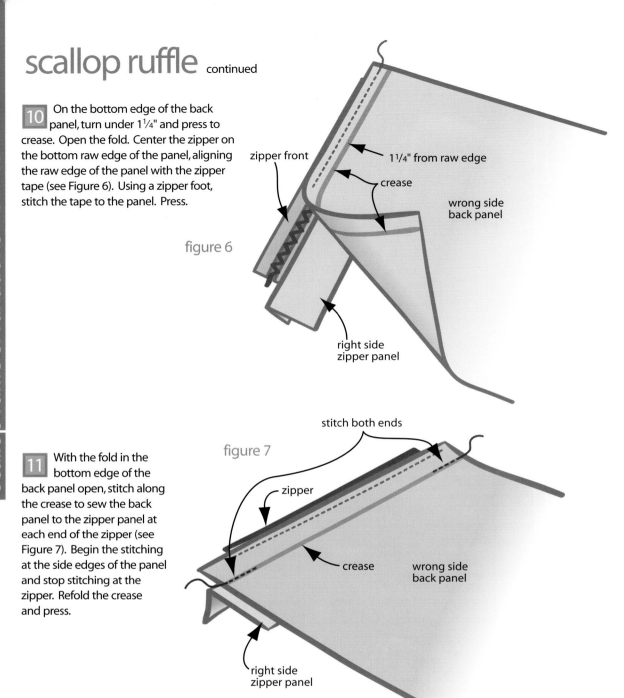

zipper front

1¼" from raw edge

crease

wrong side
back panel

figure 6

right side
zipper panel

11 With the fold in the bottom edge of the back panel open, stitch along the crease to sew the back panel to the zipper panel at each end of the zipper (see Figure 7). Begin the stitching at the side edges of the panel and stop stitching at the zipper. Refold the crease and press.

stitch both ends

figure 7

zipper

crease

wrong side
back panel

right side
zipper panel

12 Measure the zippered back panel. If the panel is larger than 17" square, trim the excess from the raw edge. Open the zipper. With right sides together and raw edges aligned, stitch the back panel to the front panel along the previous basting in the front panel, catching the scalloped units in the stitches. Pivot the stitching at the corners. Clip the corners and grade the seam allowance. Press the seam.

13 Turn to the right side through the zipper. Press the seams. To remove the visible lines of gathering stitches in the scalloped units, pull the bobbin thread and then the top thread. Because the stitches are locked and knotted, you may need to use a seam ripper to pull a few stitches from the fabric. Insert the pillow form into the cover through the zipper. Close the zipper.

prairie points:

Instead of scallops, trim your pillow with a border of folded triangles. This traditional quilt border can evoke country charm or, in bold fabrics, the Art Deco Era of the 1920s and 1930s.

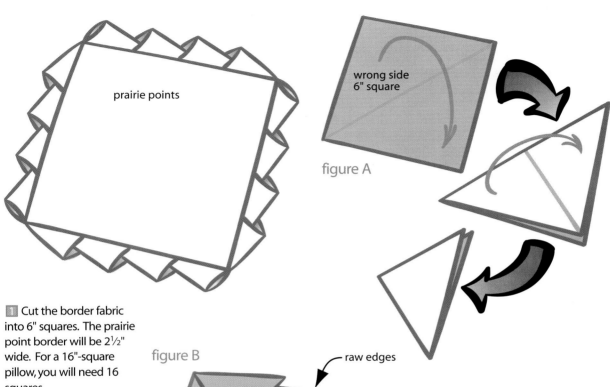

prairie points

wrong side
6" square

figure A

1 Cut the border fabric into 6" squares. The prairie point border will be 2½" wide. For a 16"-square pillow, you will need 16 squares.

2 With wrong sides together, fold each square in half from corner to corner. Press. Fold in half again, matching raw edges, and press (see Figure A).

3 Arrange the points along the raw edges of the front panel, overlapping the points 2½" to 3". Slip each point into the point next to it (see Figure B).

4 Pin 4 points to each side of the front panel. At the corners, place the edges of the triangles side by side (see Figure C). Baste in place, then assemble the pillow following Steps 9–13.

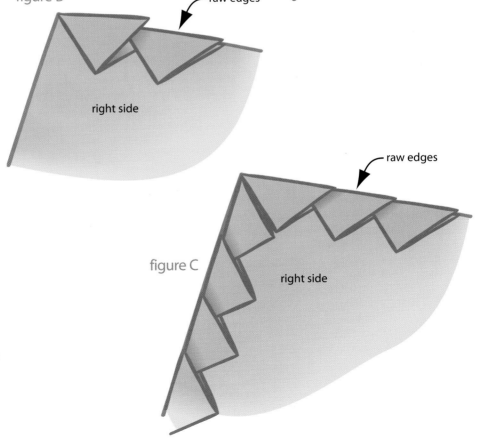

figure B

raw edges

right side

figure C

raw edges

right side

tabs: Simple fabric tabs, such as those on tab-top curtains, can form a checkerboard border on toss pillows. Alternate fabrics to make a check design, or leave an open space between the tabs as shown below.

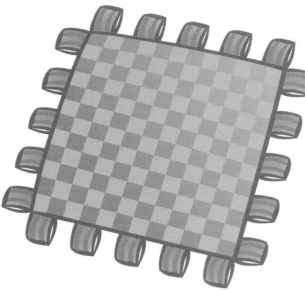

1 To make a tab edging for a 16" pillow, cut 20 (5") squares. With right sides together and raw edges aligned, fold each tab in half. Orient the fabric in the same direction on each tab. Using a 1/2" seam allowance, stitch the long raw edges together, forming a tube. Press the seam open. Turn the tab to the right side. Center the seam on the back of the tube and press flat (see Figure A). Repeat for remaining tabs.

2 With the seam sides together and raw edges aligned, fold each tab in half. Press. On the right side of the front panel, with raw edges aligned, position 1 tab 1/2" from each end of the side edge. Evenly space 3 more tabs between those on the ends. Using a 1/2" seam allowance and a long stitch length, baste the tabs to the front panel (see Figure B).

figure A

figure B

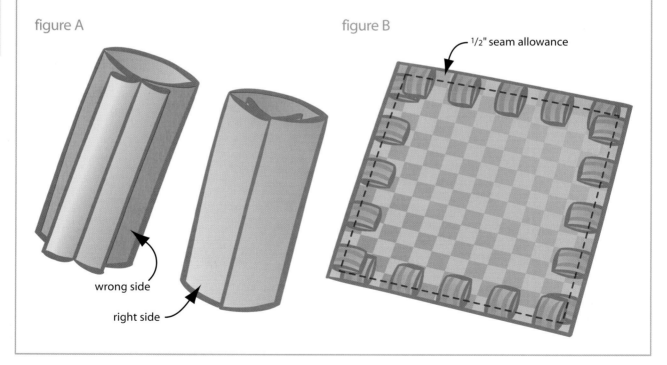

1/2" seam allowance

wrong side

right side

ribbon fringe:

A froth of ribbon fringe creates a luxurious effect. Choose at least 3 coordinating ribbon patterns in 3 different textures and widths. You will build this fringe on the back panel from the bottom up. Start with the widest ribbon and work to the narrowest ribbon.

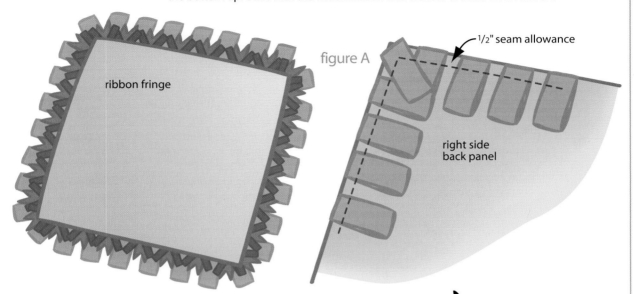

ribbon fringe

figure A

½" seam allowance

right side
back panel

1 To make a 3"-wide fringe on a 16"-square pillow, purchase 6 yards of 2"-wide ribbon, 5 yards of 1½"-wide ribbon, and 8 yards of narrow ribbon.

2 Cut the wide ribbon into 7" lengths. Fold each length in half, matching the cut ends. Pin the ribbon tabs to the right side of the back panel, aligning raw edges. Fit additional tabs around the corners. Using a ½" seam allowance, baste the ribbons to the back panel, pivoting the stitching at the corners (see Figure A).

3 Cut the medium-width ribbon into 2½" lengths. Cut one end of each ribbon at an angle or in a V-shape (see Figure B). Apply liquid ravel preventer to the cut ends and let dry. Place the medium-width ribbon pieces over the gaps between the wide ribbons, aligning raw edges. Baste along the previous basting line.

4 Cut the narrow ribbon into 4½" lengths. Apply liquid ravel preventer to the cut ends and let dry. Fold each length in half at the center, slightly skewing the ribbon ends to make a V shape (see Figure C). Place these pieces over the medium ribbon, arranging them evenly around the edges of the panel and aligning the fold with the raw edge of the panel. Baste along the previous basting.

5 Check the fringe by turning the seam allowance to the wrong side of the back panel and placing the front panel over the back panel, wrong sides together. Add more ribbon to the fringe, as desired, then assemble (see pages 59–60).

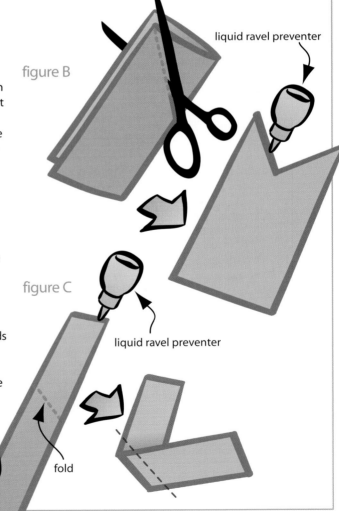

figure B

liquid ravel preventer

figure C

liquid ravel preventer

fold

Sculpted pillow shapes add a playful note to any setting.

The shape that works best for you is a matter of personal preference—easy-to-draw designs include stars, hearts, stylized birds, or simple fish. Choose fabric to suit your style too. A seersucker plaid stitched into a star has a lighthearted look; the same shape in velveteen would make a dressy accent for the holidays.

shaped pillow

Shaped pillows are ideal for children's rooms. Repeat a theme from the bedding or wallpaper with simple cutout shapes, such as fish or flowers. Enrich the design with surface details: Use the machine to satin-stitch eyes, fins, or scales on a fish, or petals and textured centers on flower-shape cushions.

A shaped pillow also can accent a theme or add a spirit of fun in other rooms. In the family room, for example, underscore an Americana theme with stars made from ticking or stripes. For the bed, make a plump star from chenille or soft terrycloth.

Shaped pillows do require that you design your own pattern. If you're not confident of your artistic abilities, use the simple drawings in children's coloring books as patterns. Eliminate any thin lines and keep divided areas as wide as possible. In the star, for example, the points are wider than they are long. For a flower pattern, make the petals with shallow but distinct dips in the outer edge of the pattern to keep it as simple as possible.

materials

14"-square paper
18" square of 2"-thick
   upholstery foam
Permanent marker
Polyester batting
3/4 yard 54"-wide
   decorator fabric
Dry-cleaning bag

tools

Electric knife, utility knife, or
   serrated knife

sewing tools

Sewing machine
Iron and ironing board
Fabric marking pen or pencil
Pins
Needles
Thread
Scissors
Tape measure
Liquid ravel preventer

skill level: advanced
time required: 8 hours

shaped pillow:

1 From paper, cut a pattern for a star or other desired shape. Place the pattern on the foam and draw around the pattern with a permanent marker. Remove the paper. Using an electric knife, utility knife, or serrated knife, cut out the star along the marked lines.

2 Using the pattern as a guide, cut 2 star-shape pieces and one long 3"-wide strip from batting. Center the strip over the side edges of the foam star, fitting the batting into the corners and folding the excess onto the top and bottom surfaces of the star. Place 1 star-shape batting piece on the top of the foam star, aligning the edges. Using a needle and thread, stitch the batting strip to the batting star by hand (see Figure 1). Stitch the remaining star-shape batting piece to the bottom of the foam in the same manner.

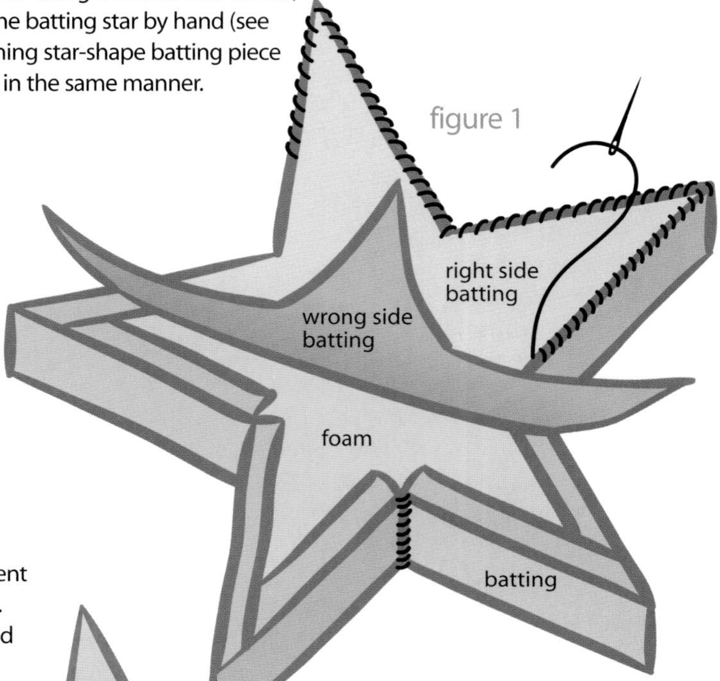

figure 1

right side
batting

wrong side
batting

foam

batting

3 Place the pattern on the fabric, centering any prominent motif. Mark a 1/2" seam allowance around the pattern. Cut 1 star panel, then reposition the pattern and cut a second star panel. Measure the edges of the pattern and add a 2" seam allowance to determine the cut length of the gusset. From fabric, cut a 3"-wide strip to this length for the gusset.

4 On one end of the gusset, turn under 1/2". Press. With right sides together, raw edges aligned, and beginning at one point of the bottom star panel, pin the gusset to the panel between the first 2 points. Clip the seam allowance of the gusset at the corners. Position the pins on the wrong side of the gusset to sew the seam from that side of the fabric (see Figure 2). Using a 1/2" seam allowance and a long stitch length, baste the gusset to the bottom panel. Pivot the stitching at the corners. Pin the gusset to the bottom panel between the next pair of star points and stitch in the same manner.

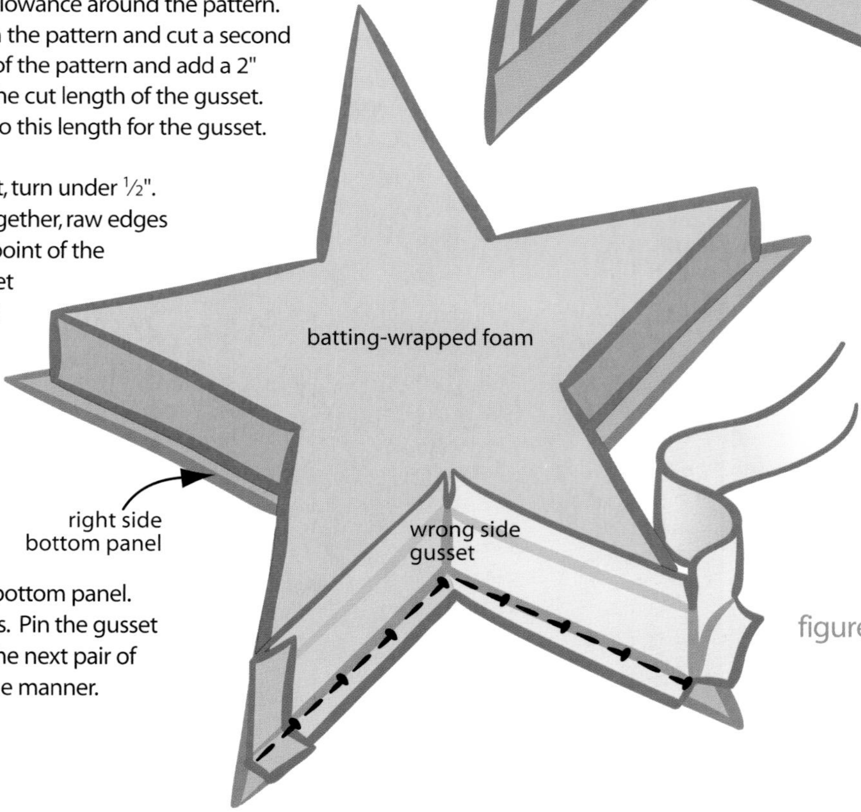

batting-wrapped foam

right side
bottom panel

wrong side
gusset

figure 2

5 Continue pinning and stitching until the gusset ends meet. Lap the end over the folded beginning edge (see Figure 3). Trim the excess gusset. Turn the seam to the right side. Check for puckers in the seam on the gusset or bottom panel and restitch if necessary.

6 With right sides together and raw edges aligned, pin the gusset to the top star panel. Position the pins on the wrong side of the top panel to sew the seam from that side of the gusset. Clip the seam allowance of the gusset at the corners. Working in this manner, both sides of the gusset will be stitched in the same direction, alleviating pulling or rippling on the gusset in the finished pillow. Using a ½" seam allowance and a long stitch length, baste the gusset to the top panel, leaving an opening in the seam between 2 star points where the gussets meet. Pivot the stitching at the corners. Turn to the right side and check the seam for puckers. Restitch if necessary.

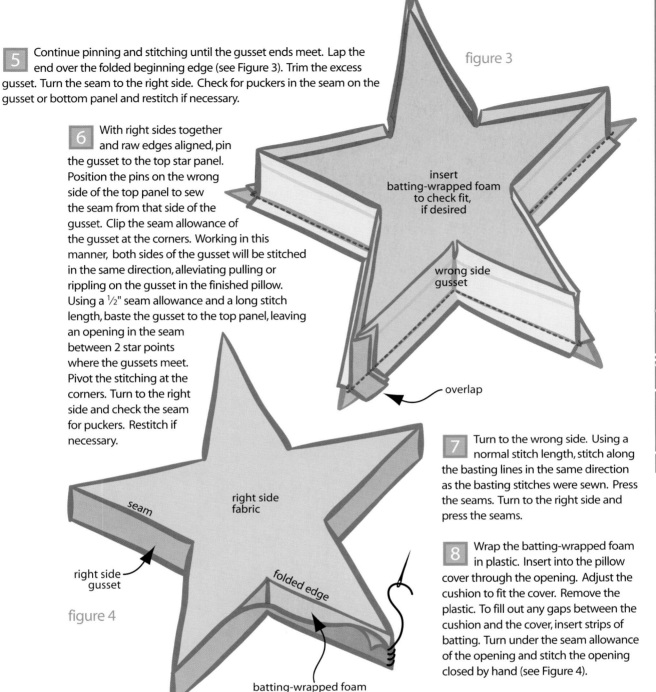

figure 3

insert batting-wrapped foam to check fit, if desired

wrong side gusset

overlap

right side fabric

seam

right side gusset

figure 4

folded edge

batting-wrapped foam

7 Turn to the wrong side. Using a normal stitch length, stitch along the basting lines in the same direction as the basting stitches were sewn. Press the seams. Turn to the right side and press the seams.

8 Wrap the batting-wrapped foam in plastic. Insert into the pillow cover through the opening. Adjust the cushion to fit the cover. Remove the plastic. To fill out any gaps between the cushion and the cover, insert strips of batting. Turn under the seam allowance of the opening and stitch the opening closed by hand (see Figure 4).

TECHNIQUES MADE EASY

it's a tight fit

Gusset pillow covers are meant to fit the underlying foam cushion as closely as possible. To fit the cover to the cushion, wrap the foam in a layer of batting. The batting makes it easier to adjust the shape of the pillow form to that of the cover because it fills out any excess space if the cover is slightly loose and compresses easily if the cover is tighter than expected in some places.

When it is time to insert the cushion into the fabric cover, loosely wrap the cushion in a dry cleaning bag. This makes a slick surface to slide into the cover. Once you have fit the cushion into the cover, pull one edge of the plastic until it slips from between the cushion and the cover. To adjust the cushion farther, lay your hand inside the plastic and then slide your hand between the cushion and cover.

The name of this little bedroom pillow comes from its function as much as its form. Originally, these firm, cylinder-shaped pillows were tucked under a bed pillow to give extra support to the neck. Now they are more often decorative than functional, providing a contrasting shape on a well-made bed.

neckroll pillow

Take the neckroll's decorative significance into account when choosing fabrics and trims. You may design it to match the bedding, as shown *at left*, or you may prefer to choose coordinating fabrics and trims. Because the pillows are small, you can indulge in luxurious fabrics, if you wish. Choose a faux animal skin, for example, or a lush silk, velvet, or chenille, or combine several rich fabrics on one pillow.

The pillow's original function is still worth remembering. If you find yourself scrunching a feather pillow into a shape you can tuck under your neck, consider making some small neckroll pillow covers in soft, washable cotton—or use inexpensive pillowcases to make removable covers. In a guestroom, be sure to outfit the bed with one of these functional neckroll pillows per sleeper.

6"×16" neckroll pillow form
³/₄ yard 54"-wide decorator
   fabric (toile)
³/₄ yard 54"-wide
   complementary decorator
   fabric (ticking)
³/₄ yard 54"-wide accent
   decorator fabric (check)
1¼ yards decorative braid or
   gimp
2 (1¼"-diameter) buttons to
   cover
1¼ yards ⁶/₃₂" filler cord

sewing tools

Sewing machine
Iron and ironing board
Fabric marking pen or pencil
Pins
Needles
Invisible thread
Thread
Scissors
Tape measure
Liquid ravel preventer

skill level: intermediate
time required: 5 hours

neckroll pillow:

1 From decorator fabric, cut 1 (9"×22") center panel. From complementary fabric, cut 2 (4"×22") end strips and enough 1½"-wide bias strips to equal 1¼ yards. From accent fabric, cut 2 (5"×22") side panels.

2 With right sides faceup, lay out the center panel with the side panels along each long edge. With right sides together and raw edges aligned, stitch 1 side panel to each long edge of the center panel, using a ½" seam allowance. Press the seams open.

3 On the right side of the fabrics, place braid over the seam lines. Thread the upper portion of the sewing machine with invisible thread and load conventional thread on the bobbin. Using a long stitch length, topstitch the braid to the panels, covering the seam. Stitch each edge of the braid in the same direction, rather than stitching down one edge and up the other (see Figure 1). Turn the panel to the wrong side. Press the stitches.

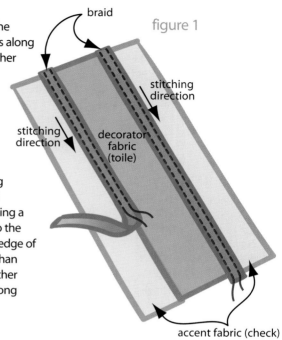

braid

figure 1

stitching direction

stitching direction

decorator fabric (toile)

accent fabric (check)

4 With right sides together and raw edges aligned, pin the top and bottom edges of the panel together. Match the ends of the braid along the edge. Using a ½" seam allowance and normal stitch length, stitch the edges together. Press the seam open and turn the resulting tube to the right side. Cover the seam with a pressing cloth; steam the seam and lightly press (see Figure 2).

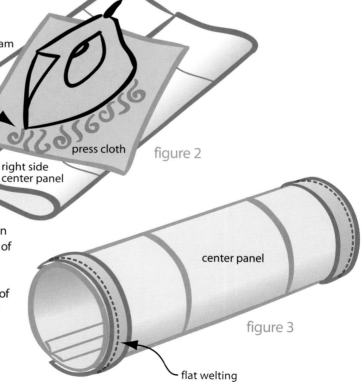

steam the seam

press cloth

right side center panel

figure 2

center panel

flat welting

figure 3

5 To make welting, fold the bias strip around the cord, wrong sides together, matching the long raw edges. Using a zipper foot and long stitch length, baste close to the cord, encasing the cord in the fabric cover. Pin the welting to the right side of each end of the center tube with raw edges aligned. Where the welting ends meet, overlap them 1". Remove the stitching from the fabric cover on each end. Unfold the fabric and cut the ends of the cord to meet. Refold 1 end of the cover over the cord. On the remaining end, turn the cover under ½" and refold the fabric around the cord, concealing the raw ends of the fabric cover. Using a zipper foot and long stitch length, baste the welting to each end of the center tube (see Figure 3). Set the tube aside.

6 With right sides together and raw edges aligned, match the short ends of each end strip. Using a ¹/₂" seam allowance, stitch each pair of edges together, forming loops. Press the seams open.

7 On 1 raw edge of each loop, make 4 lines of gathering stitches ³/₄", ¹/₂", ³/₈", and ¹/₄" from the raw edge. Stitch all lines of gathering stitches in the same direction.

8 With right sides together and raw edges aligned, pin the remaining edge of 1 end loop to each end of the center tube. Using a zipper foot, stitch the end loops to the tube following the previous basting stitches for the welting. Press the seam and grade the seam allowances. Turn the seam to the center tube. Turn the cover to the right side (see Figure 4).

9 Insert the neckroll pillow form into the cover. Position the ends of the form even with the seams with welting. On each end of the cover, pull up the bobbin threads of all 4 gathering lines to gather the fabric. Make the gathers as tight as possible. Turn ¹/₂" to the inside of the cover at the center of the gathers on each end. Adjust the gathers. Using a needle and thread, make stitches across the center of the gathered edge by hand to secure the shape (see Figure 5).

10 Cover the buttons with accent fabric following the manufacturer's instructions. Sew 1 button to each end at the center of the gathers.

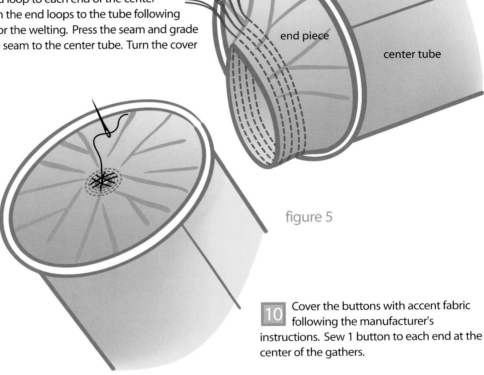

figure 4

end piece

center tube

figure 5

MORE GOOD IDEAS

no-sew neckroll

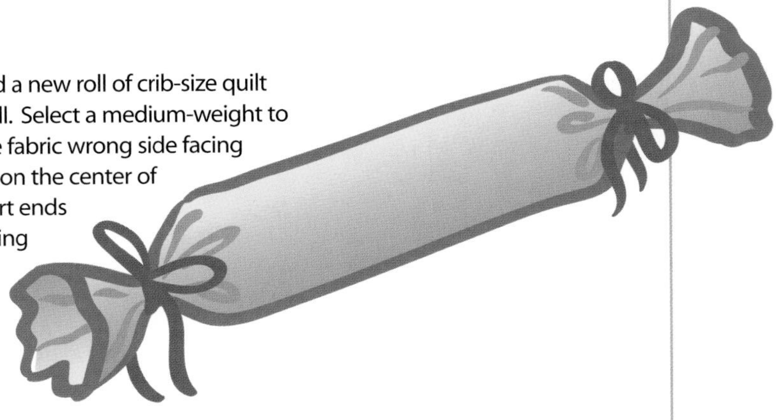

In half an hour, using ¹/₂ yard of fabric and a new roll of crib-size quilt batting, you can fashion a no-sew neckroll. Select a medium-weight to lightweight fabric for this project. Lay the fabric wrong side facing up. Place the batting, still in the package, on the center of one long edge of the fabric. Fold the short ends of the fabric to meet the ends of the batting package. Press the folds to crease.

Turn under one long edge 2" and press the fold to crease. Remove the batting roll from the packaging. Place the roll of batting on the center of the remaining raw edge of the fabric. Roll the batting in the fabric. Gather the fabric at each end of the batting and secure the ends with rubber bands. Tie ribbons over the rubber bands to finish the pillow.

materials

6"×14" neckroll pillow
¹/₂ yard 54"-wide decorator
 fabric
¹/₄ yard 54"-wide accent
 decorator fabric
1 yard ³/₈"-wide ribbon

sewing tools

Sewing machine
Iron and ironing board
Fabric marking pen or pencil
Thread
Pins
Needles
Scissors
Liquid ravel preventer
Tape measure

skill level: intermediate
time required: 4½ hours

1 From fabric, cut 1 (16"×20") center panel and cut 2 (5"×20") end panels. With right sides together and raw edges aligned, match the long edges of the center panel. Using ¹/₂" seam allowances, stitch the raw edges together, forming a tube. Press the seam open. On each end of the tube, divide the raw edges into 4 equal sections. Mark the sections with pins. Set aside the center tube.

2 With right sides together and raw edges aligned, match the short ends of the end panels, forming a loop. Using a ¹/₂" seam allowance, stitch the edges together, stopping the stitches 1" from the end to facilitate casing. Press the seam open. Using a zigzag stitch, finish the raw edges of the casing edge of each end panel. Turn under the finished edge ⁵/₈". Press the fold. Topstitch the edge ¹/₂" from the fold to make a casing (see Figure 1).

3 From accent fabric, cut 2 (4"×40") bias strips for ruffles. With right sides together and raw edges aligned, match the short ends of each ruffle strip, forming a loop. Using a ¹/₂" seam allowance, stitch the short ends together. Press the seams open. With wrong sides together and raw edges aligned, fold each ruffle in half, matching the long raw edges. Press the fold to crease.

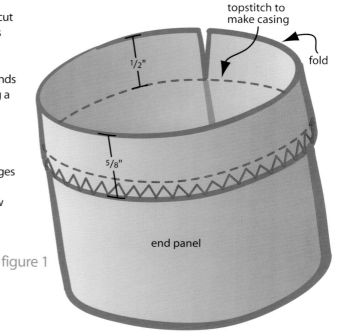

topstitch to make casing

fold

¹/₂"

⁵/₈"

end panel

figure 1

4 Treating the long raw edges of the ruffle as 1, divide the edge into 4 sections. Make 4 continuous lines of gathering stitches ³/₄", ¹/₂", ³/₈", and ¹/₄" from the raw edge. To create even gathers in the ruffle, sew all lines of gathering stitches in the same direction and keep 1 side of the ruffle on top. Mark the top side of the ruffle as the right side.

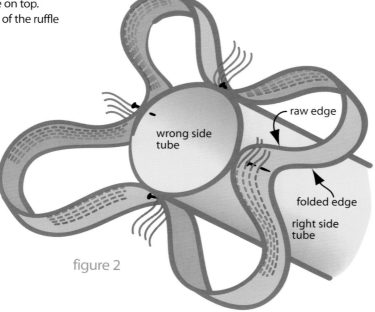

wrong side tube

raw edge

folded edge

right side tube

figure 2

5 With right sides together and raw edges aligned, match the quarter marks on 1 end of the center tube with the quarter marks on 1 ruffle (see Figure 2). On the ruffle, pull up the bobbin thread of all 4 gathering lines together to fit the ruffle to the edge of the center tube. Using a ¹/₂" seam allowance and a long stitch length, baste the ruffle to the center tube. Press the seam allowance of the ruffle. Fit and baste the remaining ruffle to the opposite end of the center tube in the same manner.

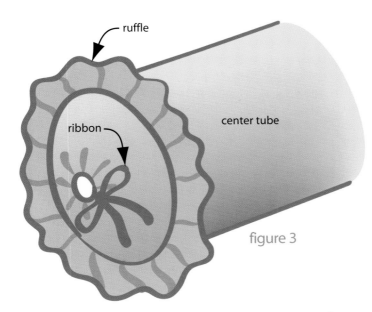

ruffle

ribbon

center tube

figure 3

6 Turn the end panels right side out. Turn the center tube wrong side out. With right sides together and raw edges aligned, slip 1 end panel inside each end of the center tube. Stitch each end following the previous basting line for the ruffle. Press the seam allowance toward the tube. Turn the cover to the right side.

7 Insert the pillow form into the cover. Cut the ribbon in half. Apply ravel preventer to the ribbon ends and let dry. Thread 1 ribbon through the casing in each end panel. Pull the ribbon ends to close the ends of the neckroll. Make a bow with the ribbon ends (see Figure 3).

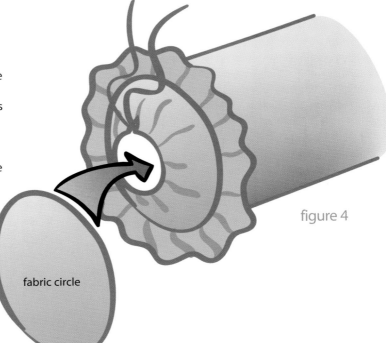

fabric circle

figure 4

8 If there is a small opening at the center of the drawstring, cut a 6"-diameter circle of fabric to tuck inside each end of neckroll to hide the pillow form (see Figure 4).

drawstring neckroll pillow how-to

The mail carrier won't deliver this parcel, so it's up to you to sew a letter-perfect pillow. An envelope pillow with its flap-front design provides an interesting focal point against an array of simple knife-edge pillows.

envelope pillow

The fringe edging and rosette on this plaid pillow impart a playful feeling that suits the casual porch setting. If the style of your room calls for simpler lines, replace the fringe in the seams of the pillow with welting made of the same fabric as the cover. Or use contrast piping for a clean edging that accents the pillow shape with color.

For a more formal setting, sew the pillow in a silky, shimmering fabric and finish the front with a tassel. Slip a beautiful glass bead or a sophisticated faux pearl on the tassel loop before stitching the tassel in place. Or use a piece of costume jewelry for a closure.

For a rustic retreat, make the pillow from soft leather, wool, or flannel plaid and close the envelope with a leather thong and a horn button. Look for soft leather at crafts stores, or use a chamois drying cloth (sold with car-care supplies). Stitch the button to the flap and the opposite end of the leather thong to the front panel.

envelope pillow:

1 From paper, cut a 24"×32" rectangle. Fold the paper in half, matching the long edges, and crease the fold. Open the fold and mark a point 4" from the corner on 1 long edge (see Figure 1). Draw an angled line from this point to the fold. Refold the paper and cut both layers along the marked line, then reopen the fold.

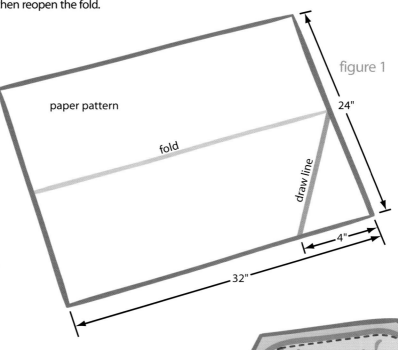

paper pattern

fold

draw line

figure 1

24"

4"

32"

2 Place the pattern on the right side of the fabric, positioning the pattern on the bias. Add a ½" seam allowance around the pattern and cut 1 back panel. Also cut a 25" square for the front panel, positioning it to take advantage of any fabric motif if desired.

3 Place the pattern on the right side of the lining, positioning it on the straight grain. Add a ½" seam allowance around the pattern and cut 1 back lining. Also cut a 25" square for the front lining.

4 Lay the back panel right side up. Pin the braided edge of the fringe to the panel, aligning the edges (see Figure 2). Gently round square corners to ease the fringe around the panel. Where the fringe ends meet, overlap the ends ½". Apply liquid ravel preventer to the cut ends and let dry. At the center of the overlap, turn the end of the fringe into the seam allowance. Using a long stitch length, baste the fringe to the panel.

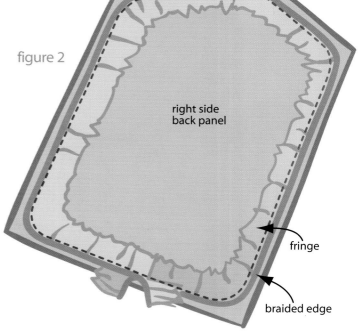

figure 2

right side
back panel

fringe

braided edge

5 Along 1 edge of the front panel, turn ½" to the wrong side (this will be the top edge). Press to crease. With right sides together and raw edges aligned, pin the front panel to back panel on the side and bottom edges. Stitch the panels together following the previous basting line in the back panel. (Be sure to keep the fringe edge out of the seam.) Clip the corners, press the seam, and turn to the right side. Press.

6 On the top edge of the front lining panel, turn under ½". Press to crease. With right sides together and raw edges aligned, pin the front lining panel to the back lining panel on the bottom and side edges. Using a ½" seam allowance, stitch the lining panels together on 3 sides, pivoting the stitching at the corners. Clip the corners and press the seams open.

7 With right sides together and raw edges aligned, pin the lining to the back panel along the edges of flap (see Figure 3). Stitch the lining to the panel following the previous basting lines in the back panel. Start and stop stitching where the front panel has been attached. Clip the corners and press the seams. Turn the flap to the right side. Press the seam. Place the fringe on the edge of the flap and press flat.

8 Tuck the lining inside the pillow cover. Align the folded edge on the front panel with the folded edge on the front lining. Edgestitch the panel and lining together along the edge. Using a needle and thread, tack the side seams in the lining to the side seams in the outer cover by hand. Insert the pillow form in the cover. Close the flap.

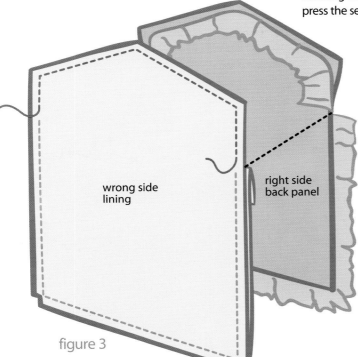

wrong side lining

right side back panel

figure 3

9 Apply liquid ravel preventer to the cut end of the fringe. To make a fringe rosette, coil fringe on a flat surface with the braid edge at the center of the circle. Make the coil as tight as possible. Using a needle and thread, tack the braid by hand to close the coil. Make a second coil by inserting braid inside the first coil with the brush end of the fringe standing up (see Figure 4). Tack the braid to itself as you work. At the center, cut the fringe. Apply ravel preventer and let dry. Tuck the end into the center of the coil. Tack the end to the braid. Sew the rosette to the right side of the flap by hand. The weight of the flap with the rosette will keep the pillow cover closed. If desired, invisibly stitch the tip of the flap to the front panel.

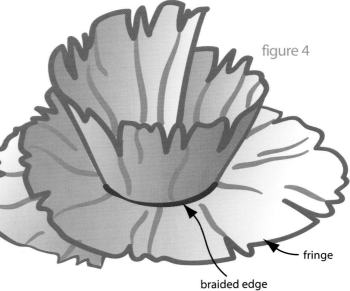

figure 4

fringe

braided edge

Round out your pillow collection with round pillows. One well-trimmed cushion can enliven the arrangement on a tailored daybed or a comfy sofa. Start with the simple hatbox-like design, *left*, and then embellish it to suit your room.

round gusset pillow

Your choice of fabric, color, and trim for the round gusset pillow will depend on the mood you want to create in the room—one of exciting contrasts or one of calm harmony. To create visual energy, sew your circular pillow in an accent color. The contrast in hue and shape will draw the eye to the little round pillow. Made from a color or fabric that blends in with the dominant color theme in the room, the round pillow makes a quieter statement, with a subtle change in shape from corners to curves.

Traditionally, the round cushion is filled with a slice of upholstery foam, which gives the pillow a firm shape. To soften the foam center, wrap the cushion in a layer of high-density polyester fiberfill batting. One layer of the high-density batting or two layers of traditional batting create a soft touch without loosening the structure provided by the upholstery foam core.

A SLICE OF FOAM

■ Slicing custom-size upholstery foam is as easy as slicing white bread. Use an electric knife, a serrated knife, or a utility knife to trim a larger piece of foam to the exact size you need. If you accidentally make a rough edge, hide the mistake with a layer of polyester batting.

■ In a modern interior, slice foam circles wafer thin to make multiple disc-like cushions for the sofa.

■ See the moon and stars on your favorite window seat with carved foam cushions made in celestial shapes.

■ Cut small circles from thick pieces of foam to fashion cylinder-shape cushions for the love seat in a whimsical attic playroom.

materials

3"-thick round upholstery
   foam 14" in diameter
Polyester fiberfill batting
1½ yards 54"-wide
   decorator fabric
3 yards $^6/_{32}$"-diameter
   filler cord
3"-diameter button to cover
Dry-cleaning bag

tools

Electric drill and drill bits
   (optional)

sewing tools

Sewing machine
Iron and ironing board
Fabric marking pen or pencil
Pins
Needles
Thread
Scissors
Tape measure
Liquid ravel preventer
Upholsterer's tufting needle
   or doll needle

skill level: beginner
time required: 6 hours

round gusset pillow:

1 Find the center of the foam circle by drawing
2 perpendicular lines across the foam. Using an electric
drill and drill bit, make a pencil-size-diameter hole through the
foam from front to back through the center (see Figure 1). Use
a skewer or a serrated kitchen knife to open the hole.

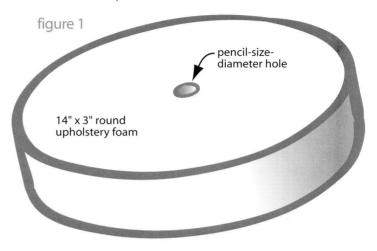

figure 1

pencil-size-
diameter hole

14" x 3" round
upholstery foam

2 From batting, cut 2 circles 15" in diameter and a 50"×3" strip to cover the
sides of the foam. Center the strip along the side edges of the foam
circle. Pin as needed to hold the batting in place. Overlap the short ends by ½"
and trim the excess. Using a needle and thread, stitch the ends together by
hand. Place 1 batting circle on top of the foam. Using a needle and thread,
stitch the batting strip to the batting circle by hand (see Figure 2). Place the
remaining batting circle on the bottom of the foam, aligning the edges and
stitch in the same manner.

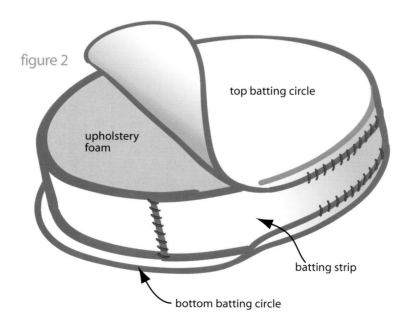

figure 2

top batting circle

upholstery
foam

batting strip

bottom batting circle

3 From fabric, cut
2 (8"×47") strips for the
pillow front and back panels.
Also from fabric, cut a 48"×4"
strip for the pillow sides. Set
the pieces aside.

4 For welting, cut enough 1¹/₂"-wide bias strips to make 3 yards. Stitch the strips together at the short ends to make a continuous length. Fold the bias strip around the filler cord, matching the long raw edges. Using a zipper foot and long stitch length, baste close to the cord, encasing the cord in the fabric cover.

5 With right sides together and raw edges aligned, pin together the short ends of the strip for the pillow side to make a continuous loop. Using a ¹/₂" seam allowance, stitch the ends together. Press the seam open. Pin the welting to the right side of the loop along 1 edge, aligning raw edges. Begin the welting away from the seam to minimize the bulk in the seam allowances. Where the welting ends meet, overlap the ends 1" and cut the welting. Remove the stitching from the fabric cover in each end. Unfold the fabric and cut the ends of the cord to meet. Refold 1 end of the cover over the cord. On the remaining end, turn the cover under ¹/₂" and refold the fabric around the cord, concealing the raw ends of the fabric cover. Using a zipper foot and a long stitch length, baste the welting to the loop. Attach welting to the remaining raw edge of the pillow side in the same manner.

6 With right sides together and raw edges aligned, pin the short ends of the panel for the pillow front to make a loop. Using a ¹/₂" seam allowance, stitch the ends together. Press the seam open. Looking at the right side of the fabric, determine which edge of the loop will be at the center of the pillow. On that edge, apply liquid ravel preventer to the cut edge and let dry. Prepare the back panel in the same manner.

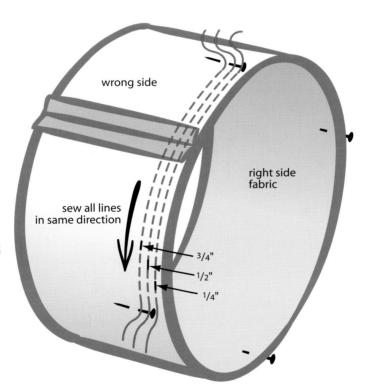

figure 3

wrong side

sew all lines in same direction

right side fabric

3/4"
1/2"
1/4"

7 Divide the treated edge on the front panel and the back panel into 4 quarters. Place pins at each quarter. Set the machine for a long stitch length and loosen the upper thread tension. Working with the wrong side of the fabric faceup and starting and stopping the stitching at each quarter mark, make 3 lines of gathering stitches ³/₄", ¹/₂", and ¹/₄" from the edge (see Figure 3). Sew all lines of gathering stitches in the same direction.

round gusset pillow continued

8 With right sides together and raw edges aligned, pin the front panel to 1 edge of the pillow side. To minimize bulk in the seam allowances, do not align the seams with each other or with the finished ends of the welting. Using a zipper foot, stitch the front panel to the pillow side following the previous basting for the welting. Keep the edge of the front panel with the gathering stitches free. Grade the seam allowances and notch the seam allowance of the front panel. Press the seam open. Pin, stitch, notch, and press the back panel to the remaining raw edge of the pillow side in the same manner as the front panel.

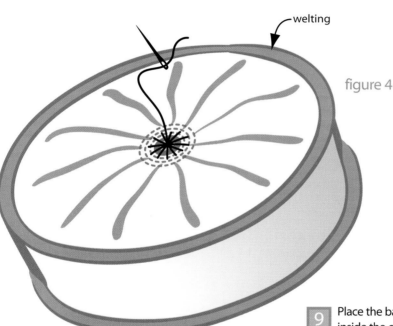

welting

figure 4

9 Place the batting-wrapped cushion inside the cover, centering the edge of the cushion between the seams with welting. On the back panel, pull up the bobbin thread (which is on the right side of the fabric) of all 3 gathering lines together. Pull the gathered edge closed and adjust it as necessary to align with the center of the cushion. Adjust the gathers, making those at the center tighter than the outer edge. Knot the thread ends together to secure the gathers. On the front panel, pull up the threads in the same manner. Knot the thread ends together. Using a needle and thread, make short stitches across the centers of the front panel and back panel to secure the gathered edges (see Figure 4).

10 Follow the manufacturer's instructions to cover the buttons with fabric. Thread the tufting needle with a double length of buttonhole thread. Knot the thread ends. Thread the needle through 1 button shank and tie the thread to the button shank. Using your fingers, press on the pillow center to find the hole made in Step 1 (page 80) through the center of the foam cushion. Pass the needle through the gathers at the pillow center from front to back through the hole in the foam cushion. Catch the shank of the remaining button (see Figure 5). Pass the needle through the pillow from back to front. Pull the thread tightly to sink the buttons into the padding of the pillow. Pass the needle through the pillow several times. Knot the thread behind 1 button. Cut the thread ends.

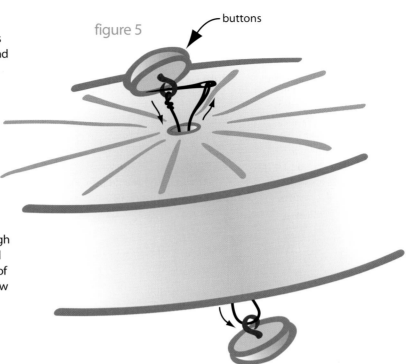

figure 5

buttons

MORE GOOD IDEAS

oversize round pillows

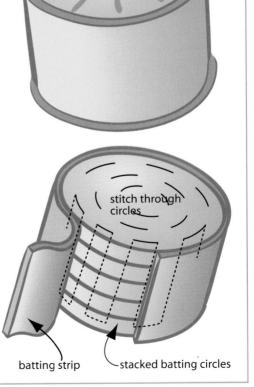

Round pillows with deep soft sides often appear in contemporary furniture settings. Sewn in lavish solid-color silks, the pillows resemble expensive, oversize chocolates or dipped candies.

To sew your own, exaggerate the depth of the basic round pillows. Plan for the depth of the pillow to be approximately two-thirds the diameter of the pillow. For your filling, stack circles of dense polyester batting to create a softer center for the pillow form. To keep the stack together, loosely stitch the layers together from top to bottom. Wrap the stack in batting in the same manner as you would the smaller foam cushion. Wrap the sides first, then cap the top and bottom of the batting cushion with slightly larger diameter circles of batting.

Because these cushions look yummiest in fine silks or velvets, use tightly woven muslin to make a cover, encasing the fibers of the batting cushion. This layer will keep the polyester fibers from working their way to the finished side of the pillow cover fabric.

stitch through circles

batting strip

stacked batting circles

Large, long, cylinder-shape pillows are called bolsters. These foam-filled cushions provide firm support for benches, sofas, and beds. On daybeds, they stand in for upholstered arms, softening the transition from the mattress to the headboard and footboard.

bolster pillow

Covering the bolsters in the same fabric that lines the bed canopy and dresses the bed creates a unified look.

The proportions of the bolster will be determined by where you plan to use it. For a daybed, use a cushion at least 9 inches in diameter and as long as the bed is deep. You have several options for finishing the bolster ends: a smooth fabric cover with deeply inset button, like those shown *at left*, is understated and formal. To make the buttoned ends, cut narrow slices off the ends of the cushion and use them to button through the fabric cover at each end. Then insert the center section into the cover to fill out the length. The center section will apply pressure to the complete assembly, making a stable cushion.

Other options (shown on pages 90 and 91) include a gathered fabric end, suited for casual or cottage-style settings, and a pleated end, ideal for a tailored guest room or sitting room.

9"×24" upholstery foam bolster
High-loft polyester upholstery batting
1³/₄ yards 54"-wide decorator fabric
³/₄ yard 54"-wide lining fabric
⁶/₃₂" filler cord
Zipper
2 (2") buttons to cover

tools

Electric knife

sewing tools

Sewing machine
Iron and ironing board
Fabric marking pen or pencil
Pins
Needles
Thread
Scissors
Tape measure
Liquid ravel preventer

skill level: advanced
time required: 8 hours

bolster pillow:

1 From batting, cut 4 (9"-diameter) circles and 1 (25"×29") panel. From lining, cut 1 (25"×29") panel. Set the batting pieces and lining aside.

2 From fabric, cut 1 (25"×32") center panel, and 2 (10"-diameter) circles for the end panels. Cut 1¹/₂ yards of 1¹/₂"-wide bias strips for welting.

3 To make welting, fold the bias strip around the cord, matching the long raw edges. Using a zipper foot and long stitch length, baste close to the cord, encasing the cord in the fabric cover. Pin the welting to the right side of each end panel, with raw edges aligned. Clip the seam allowance of the welting to ease it around each circle (see Figure 1). Where the welting ends meet, overlap the ends 1". Cut the welting. Remove the stitching from the fabric cover on each end. Unfold the fabric and cut the ends of the cord to meet. Refold 1 end of the cover over the cord. On the remaining end, turn the cover under ¹/₂" and refold the fabric around the cord, concealing the raw ends of the fabric cover. Using a zipper foot and long stitch length, baste the welting to each end panel. Set the end panels aside.

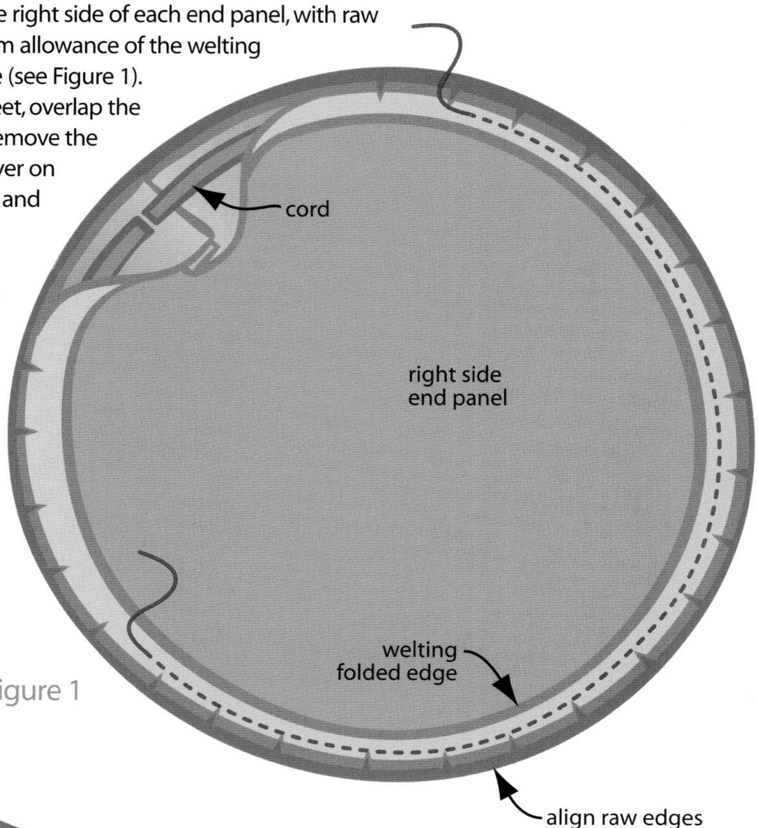

cord

right side
end panel

welting
folded edge

align raw edges

figure 1

4 On the right side of the center panel, place the zipper tab face down, centered, on 1 (25"-long) edge. Align the tape edge of the zipper with the raw edge of the panel. Using a zipper foot, stitch the zipper tape to the fabric. With right sides together and raw edges aligned at the zipper end of the panel, place the lining on the center panel. Using a zipper foot, stitch the lining to the panel, catching the zipper tape in the seam. Press the seam. Turn to the right side, placing the zipper on the edge. Press flat.

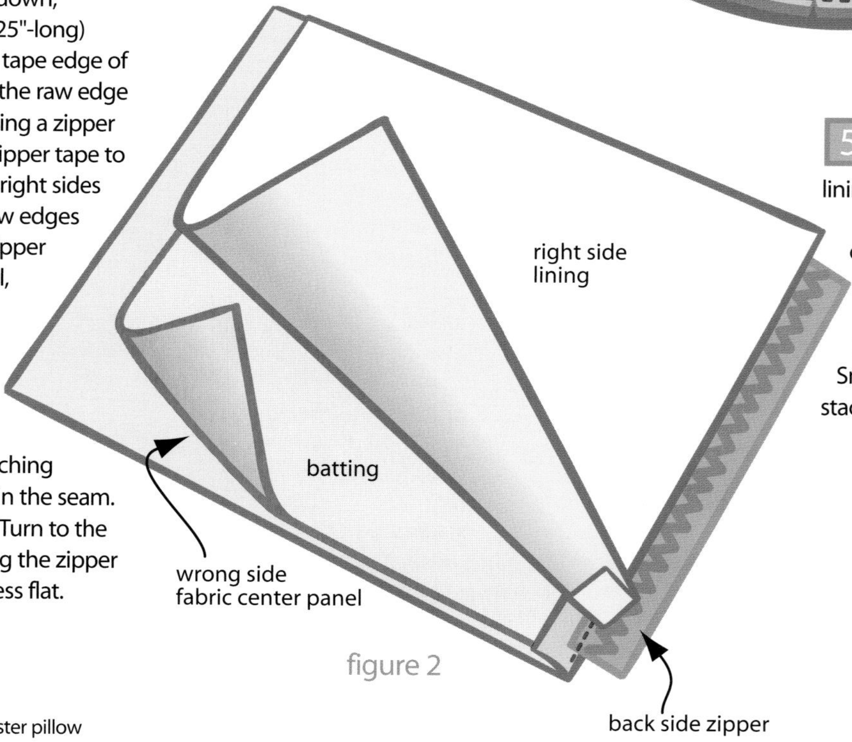

right side
lining

batting

wrong side
fabric center panel

5 Lay the center panel wrong side up. Lift the lining. With raw edges aligned, stack the batting on the wrong side of the panel. Pin the batting to the panel from the right side of the panel. Smooth the lining over the stack (see Figure 2).

figure 2

back side zipper

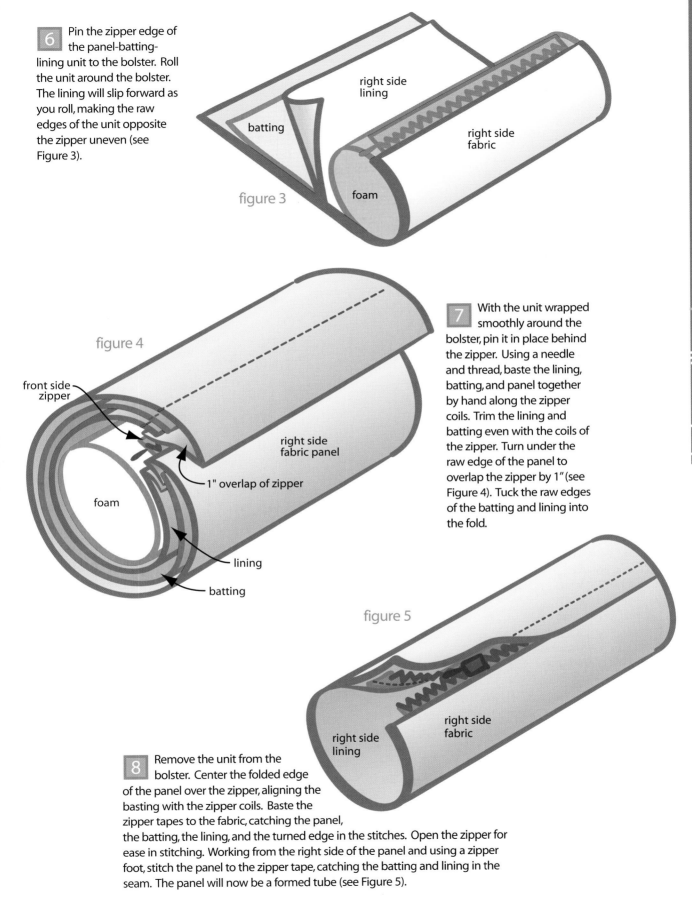

6 Pin the zipper edge of the panel-batting-lining unit to the bolster. Roll the unit around the bolster. The lining will slip forward as you roll, making the raw edges of the unit opposite the zipper uneven (see Figure 3).

figure 3

right side lining

batting

right side fabric

foam

figure 4

front side zipper

foam

1" overlap of zipper

right side fabric panel

lining

batting

7 With the unit wrapped smoothly around the bolster, pin it in place behind the zipper. Using a needle and thread, baste the lining, batting, and panel together by hand along the zipper coils. Trim the lining and batting even with the coils of the zipper. Turn under the raw edge of the panel to overlap the zipper by 1" (see Figure 4). Tuck the raw edges of the batting and lining into the fold.

figure 5

right side fabric

right side lining

8 Remove the unit from the bolster. Center the folded edge of the panel over the zipper, aligning the basting with the zipper coils. Baste the zipper tapes to the fabric, catching the panel, the batting, the lining, and the turned edge in the stitches. Open the zipper for ease in stitching. Working from the right side of the panel and using a zipper foot, stitch the panel to the zipper tape, catching the batting and lining in the seam. The panel will now be a formed tube (see Figure 5).

bolster pillow continued

9 Adjust the pressure foot to a lower weight. Using a long stitch length and working with the panel on the top side of the fabric stack, baste 1/2" from the raw edges on each end of the tube. Baste in a continuous line around each end. Turn back the panel and lining. Trim the batting from each seam allowance. Clip the seam allowances of the lining and batting.

bolster pillow how-to

10 Open the zipper. With right sides together and raw edges aligned, pin 1 end panel to each end of the tube (see Figure 6). Align the basting in the end panel with the basting in the end of the tube. Adjust the pressure foot weight. Using a zipper foot and long stitch length, baste the end panels to the tube following the previous basting lines. Turn the seam to the right side to check for puckers in either piece of fabric. Remove the stitches and adjust the seams if necessary. Using a normal stitch length, restitch each end on the basting. Grade the seam allowances. Press. Turn to the right side. Press the seams.

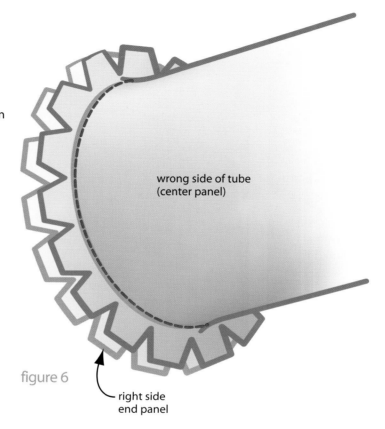

wrong side of tube (center panel)

figure 6

right side end panel

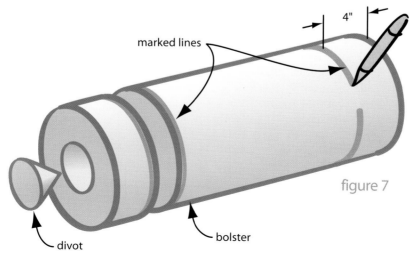

marked lines

figure 7

divot

bolster

11 On the bolster, measure 4" from each end. Using a permanent marker, mark a line around the bolster. Using an electric knife, cut the ends off the bolster following the line. The bolster will be reassembled later. The end pieces will be used to make button-tufted ends. On each end piece, mark the center. Using an electric knife, cut a cone-shaped divot from the foam at the center mark (see Figure 7).

4"

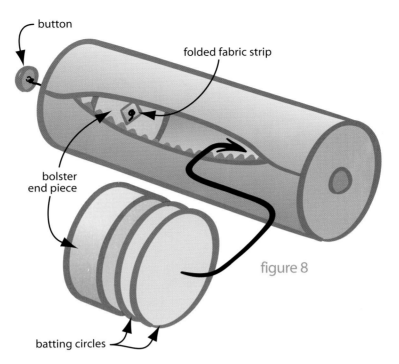

button

folded fabric strip

bolster
end piece

batting circles

figure 8

12 On each end piece of the bolster, stack 2 batting circles. Insert 1 batting/foam unit into each end of the bolster cover. Following the manufacturer's instructions, cover buttons with scraps of fabric. Using a tufting needle and doubled buttonhole thread, stitch 1 button by hand to the center of each end of the bolster cover. Pass the needle through the batting and slice of bolster foam, pulling the button deep into the padding. Use a small piece of fabric, folded into quarters, as an anchor for the stitches on the back side of the bolster slice (see Figure 8). Knot the thread ends on the back of the bolster slice.

13 Insert the center section of the bolster foam into the cover through the zipper. Align the bolster center with the bolster end slices. Close the zipper.

BOLSTER FORMS

■ Solid foam bolsters are sold through upholstery supply wholesalers. Do not hesitate to call on one of these businesses for the supplies you might need to sew for your home. They often deal directly with private individuals.

■ If you are unable to locate a source for a solid bolster, you can create a suitable foam bolster with supplies found at a local fabric store. In these stores, the foam is generally available in 24" widths. Purchase 4 yards of $1/2$"-thick foam to make a 9"×24" bolster.

■ Beginning at one short edge, roll the foam tightly; however, do not compress the foam too much. Keep the side edges of the foam even. At the end, pin the edge of the foam to the roll. Measure the diameter. Reroll, if necessary, to make the bolster smaller or larger: Looser rolling makes a larger diameter and tighter rolling makes a smaller diameter. Using a tufting needle or other large needle, make large stitches over the edge into the roll to secure the rolled shape of the bolster.

■ To make the deep-button cushion with this homemade type of bolster, purchase another yard of $1/2$"-thick foam and cut 2 (9"-diameter) circles to serve as the pieces of foam referred to as end slices in the step-by-step instructions.

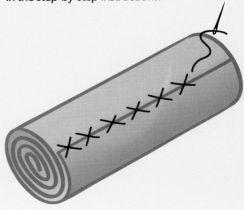

gathered ends: For a more informal setting or a cottage-style room, simply gather the bolster ends.

1 For the end panels, cut 2 (5 1/2"×28") strips. With right sides together and raw edges aligned, fold each strip, matching the short ends. Using a 1/2" seam allowance, stitch the edges together. Press the seam open.

2 On 1 raw edge of each loop, make 4 lines of gathering stitches 3/4", 1/2", 3/8", and 1/4" from the raw edge. Stitch all lines of gathering stitches in the same direction.

3 On the remaining raw edge of each loop, pin the welting, aligning the raw edges. Using a zipper foot and long stitch length, baste the welting to the end panel.

4 With right sides together and raw edges aligned, pin 1 end piece to each end of the center tube. Using a zipper foot, stitch following the previous basting stitches in the tube and end piece. Press the seam. Grade the seam allowances. Turn to the right side and press the seam.

5 On each end, pull up the bobbin threads of all 4 gathering lines to gather the fabric (see Figure A). Make the gathers as tight as possible. Insert the full bolster into the cover and close the zipper. The bolster will stabilize the ends of the bolster cover as you finish the gathered ends. Turn 1/2" to the inside of the cover at the center of the gathers on each end. Adjust the gathers. Using a needle and thread, make stitches across the center of the gathered edge by hand to secure the shape (see Figure B).

6 Cover buttons with scraps of accent fabric following the manufacturer's instructions. Sew 1 button to each end at the center of the gathers.

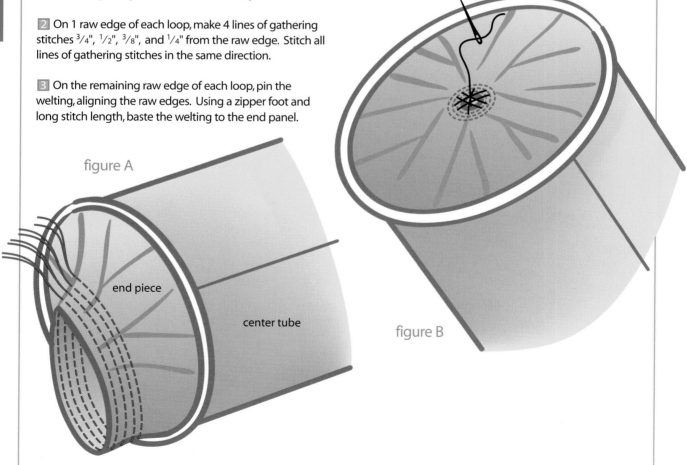

figure A

end piece

center tube

figure B

bolster pillow how-to

pleated ends: In a tailored or formal setting, pleated ends capped by an oversize button offer classic style.

1 For the end panels, cut 2 (5$\frac{1}{2}$"×28") strips and 2 (10"-diameter) circles. With right sides together and raw edges aligned, fold each strip, matching the short ends. Using a $\frac{1}{2}$" seam allowance, stitch the edges together. Press the seam open.

2 On the right side of the loop, with raw edges aligned, pin the welting. Using a zipper foot and long stitch length, baste the welting to the end panel.

3 Turn the loop right side out. With the wrong side of the loop to the right side of the circle, pin each loop to a circle (see Figure A). Clip the seam allowance of the loop and welting to ease the piece around the circle. Using a zipper foot and long stitch length, baste the loop and welting to the circle.

4 Make pleats in the remaining raw edge of the loop to bring the ends together at the center of the circle. Turn under the exposed raw edges. Using a needle and thread, make stitches by hand to secure the pleats at the center (see Figure B). Use the underlying circle piece to stabilize the shape. Cover the buttons with fabric scraps following the manufacturer's instructions. Stitch a button to the center of each end piece by hand, catching the circle layer in the stitches.

5 With right sides together and raw edges aligned, pin 1 end piece to each end of the center tube. Open the zipper. Clip the seam allowances of the tube to ease the tube edges around the circle-shaped end pieces. Using a zipper foot, stitch along the previous basting stitches in the tube and each end piece. Press the seams and grade the seam allowances. Turn to the right side and press the seams. Insert a 9"-diameter circle of batting in each end of the cover, then insert the bolster into the cover and close the zipper.

bolster pillow how-to

figure A

right side circle

folded edge welting

right side loop

wrong side loop

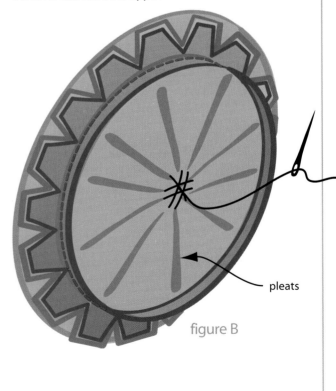

pleats

figure B

Plump your hammock or outdoor seating with these perky pillows. Seersucker plaid suits the playful spirit of the tied corners, but the design also lends itself to small florals or textured solids. Choose medium-weight to lightweight fabrics; heavy or stiff ones won't knot as tightly as required.

knotted corner pillow

A zippered closure hidden in the side seam makes it possible to remove these pillow covers for cleaning—or to replace a cushion if the pillows are caught in the rain accidentally. Weatherproof fabrics are available in a limited range of colors and patterns. Ask your fabric retailer for information. If you choose ordinary decorator fabric, protect it from dust, stains, and rain with a commercially available water-repellent spray.

To keep your backyard furnishings fresh, plan to store the cushions each evening. Simple storage solutions include large wicker baskets placed just inside the patio door or covered plastic totes stashed in the garage. New, lidded trash cans make excellent outdoor storage if you place the cans in a protected corner of the house.

materials

Newsprint or paper
14"-square pillow form
2 yards 54"-wide decorator fabric
12" invisible zipper

sewing tools

Sewing machine
Thread
Pins
Needles
Scissors
Tape measure
Fabric marking pen or pencil
Iron and ironing board
Liquid ravel preventer

skill level: intermediate
time required: 3½ hours

knotted corner pillow:

1 To make a pattern for the ties, cut a 4"×6"-piece of paper. Fold it in half, matching the long edges. Cut out a tall, narrow paper heart (see Figure 1) and set it aside. Fold a large sheet of paper in half and in half again. Measure 7" on each edge from the folded corner (see Figure 1). Draw a box, then draw a diagonal line from the folded corner extending 10" beyond the corner of the box. On each side of the diagonal line, measure and mark a line 1½" from the diagonal. Place the paper heart so the pointed tip is on the end of the diagonal and trace around the heart. Referring to Figure 1, connect the heart, diagonals, and square to make one-fourth of the pattern. Holding the folded layers of paper together, cut through all layers to make a complete pattern.

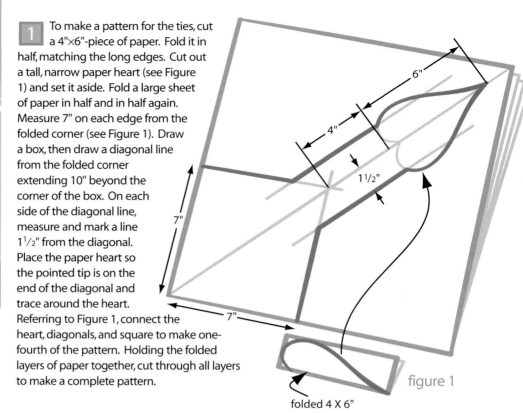

6"
4"
1½"
7"
7"

figure 1

folded 4 X 6"

2 Open the pattern and place it on the right side of the fabric. Align the pattern's diagonal line from corner to corner with the straight grain of the fabric. Add a ½" seam allowance around the pattern (see Figure 2). Mark the placement of stripes or plaids on the pattern edge to help in matching the fabric design across the seams. Cut 1 front panel. Turn the pattern facedown on the fabric again. Match the marks on the pattern to the fabric design so patterns will match across the seams. Add a ½" seam allowance around the pattern and cut out 1 back panel.

3 Lay the panels right side up with the edges for the zipper side by side. Center the zipper on the raw edge of each panel. Install the zipper following the manufacturer's instructions.

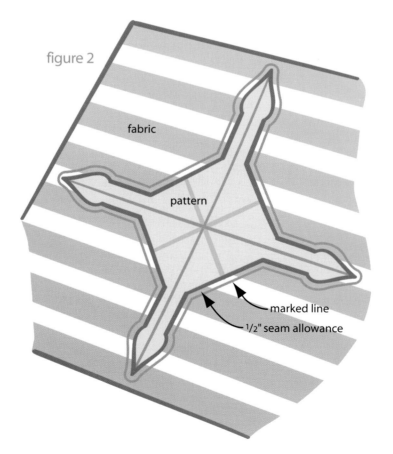

figure 2

fabric

pattern

marked line
½" seam allowance

4 With right sides together, raw edges aligned, and the fabric design matched, pin the side edges of the front and back panels. Using a ¹/₂" seam allowance, stitch the edges together. Trim the seam allowance around the curve of the extensions to ¹/₄". Clip the curves. Clip the seam allowance into the corners. Press the seam open. Turn to the right side. Press the seam.

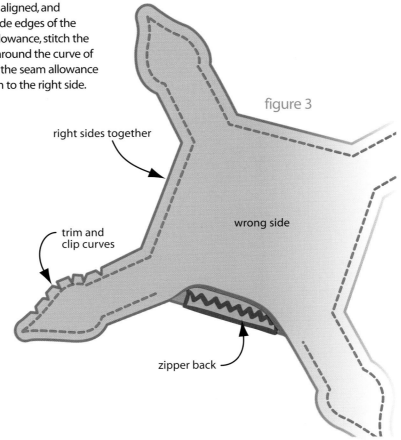

figure 3

right sides together

trim and clip curves

wrong side

zipper back

5 With right sides together, raw edges aligned, and the fabric design matched, pin the raw edges of the front panel to back panels on either side of the zipper. Using a zipper foot and ¹/₂" seam allowance, stitch the seam at each end of the zipper. Clip the curves and the seam allowance into the corners. Press the seam open. Turn to the right side. Press the seam. On the extensions, place the seam on the edge and press the extensions flat.

6 Open the zipper. With right sides together, raw edges aligned, and the fabric design matched, pin the remaining raw edges together. Using a ¹/₂" seam allowance, stitch the front panel to the back panel, pivoting the stitching at the ends of the extensions. Trim the seam allowance around the curves of the extensions to ¹/₄". Clip the curves and the seam allowance into the corners. Press the seam open and turn to the right side. Press the seam. On the extensions, place the seam on the edge and press the extensions flat.

7 Insert the pillow into the cover through the opening. Close the zipper. Make a knot in each extension. Place the knot at the base of the curved portion of the extension.

TECHNIQUES MADE EASY

how to shorten a zipper: Zipper lengths vary, but sometimes you still need to adjust them.

1 To custom-size a zipper, buy any length longer than the size you need. Set the machine for a wide stitch with 0 length. Drop or lower the feed dog if your sewing machine offers that feature.

2 Measure the length of zipper you need along the coils. At the bottom of the measured length, tack across the coils.

Move down ¹/₄" below the first tack and tack again. Cut off the bottom end of the zipper.

3 The thread tacks will work in the same way the manufacturer's zipper stop acts, preventing the zipper slide from zipping off the bottom of the coils. Install the shortened zipper in the usual manner.

Change the look of a pillow in an instant with button-on panels.

A simple, solid-color pillow is best because the plain background will serve as a frame for the panels you attach. The panels are easy to make and can reflect holidays, the seasons, or an updated color scheme.

button-on panel

Start your panel collection with a simple scrap of coordinating fabric that you used elsewhere in the room. The check fabric, *opposite*, brings together the room's blue-yellow-lime color scheme. For a more graphic effect, a solid yellow or lime panel could replace the check.

Choose fabrics of similar weight and texture for the pillow and button-on panel. Cotton-blend decorator fabrics are an obvious choice, but don't overlook the decorative possibilities of other fabrics as well. A tapestry-weight panel on a wool or velvet pillow would look luxurious and rich, as would a velveteen panel on a chenille pillow. Consider sheer fabrics as well—often they are printed or embroidered with beautiful designs or motifs. Sort through old linens at the flea markets for pieces of vintage tablecloths, napkins, tea towels, and handkerchiefs.

As a timesaving alternative to sewing the pillow, start with solid decorator pillows in cotton or chenille and choose coordinating fabric to embellish them. Look for vintage buttons at antiques stores or flea markets to add extra personality.

button-on panel:

1 From fabric, cut one 19½" square for the front panel and 2 (12" × 19½") pieces for the back panels.

2 On the right side of one back panel, center the zipper facedown on one long edge of the panel (see Figure 1). Align the zipper tape with the raw edge. Using a zipper foot, stitch the zipper tape to the panel. Turn the zipper to the right side, turning the seam allowance under the panel. Press.

3 On one long edge of the remaining back panel, turn under 1¼". Press the fold to crease. Open the fold. Center the zipper on the raw edge, aligning the raw edge of the panel with the zipper tape. Using a zipper foot, stitch the tape to the panel (see Figure 2). Press.

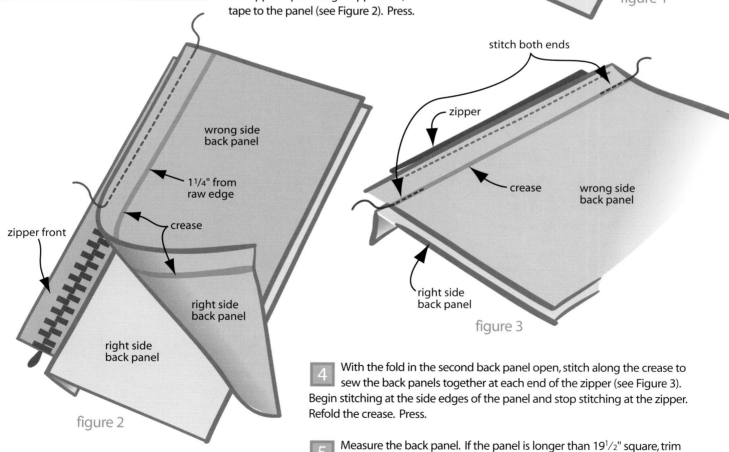

figure 1

figure 2

figure 3

4 With the fold in the second back panel open, stitch along the crease to sew the back panels together at each end of the zipper (see Figure 3). Begin stitching at the side edges of the panel and stop stitching at the zipper. Refold the crease. Press.

5 Measure the back panel. If the panel is longer than 19½" square, trim the excess, placing the zipper at the center of the panel. Open the zipper. With right sides together and raw edges aligned, pin the back panels to the front panel. Using a ½" seam allowance, stitch the panels together. Pivot the stitching at the corners. Clip the corners and grade the seam allowance. Press the seams open as far as possible into the corners.

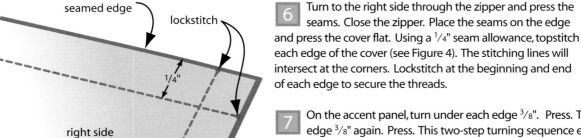

seamed edge

lockstitch

1/4"

right side panel

1/4"

seamed edge

figure 4

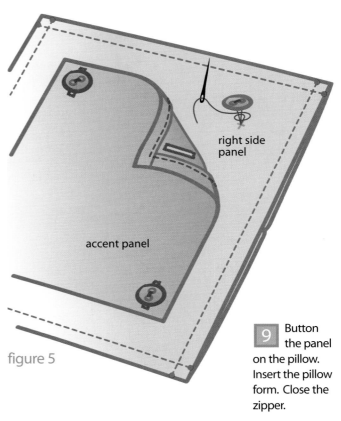

right side panel

accent panel

figure 5

6 Turn to the right side through the zipper and press the seams. Close the zipper. Place the seams on the edge and press the cover flat. Using a 1/4" seam allowance, topstitch each edge of the cover (see Figure 4). The stitching lines will intersect at the corners. Lockstitch at the beginning and end of each edge to secure the threads.

7 On the accent panel, turn under each edge 3/8". Press. Turn under each edge 3/8" again. Press. This two-step turning sequence encases all raw edges in the hems. Using a 1/4" seam allowance, topstitch each edge, pivoting the stitching at the corners. At each corner, make a machine-worked buttonhole for a 1/2" button.

8 Center the panel on the pillow front. Mark the placement of the buttons through the buttonholes. Remove the panel. Stitch 1 button to each mark on the pillow front (see Figure 5). To attach buttons properly, sew 4 to 6 loops through the button and fabric with the button lifted 1/8" to 1/4" off fabric. Bring the needle and thread to the right side under the button. Wrap the threads 4 to 6 times, making a shank. Knot the thread behind the button.

9 Button the panel on the pillow. Insert the pillow form. Close the zipper.

MORE GOOD IDEAS

plethora of panels

Once you start making panels for your button-on panel pillow, you'll need to find a deep and wide drawer to store all the designs. Look for interesting fabrics from which you can make panels, but also be inspired by other sources of designs.

Have your local copy center make color photocopies of your children's artwork on heat-transfer paper. Many of these centers will press the design onto fabric for you as well, or you can do that at home. Your family snapshots or photocopies of old handwritten letters or documents can be transferred in this same way or with a chemical product purchased at your crafts store. (Remember that photocopy centers will not reproduce copyrighted materials, which includes portraits done by professional photographers.)

Try your hand at fabric painting to produce images for your pillow panels. Use fabric paint and follow the manufacturer's instructions regarding preparation of the fabric, application of the paint, drying times, and making the finished paint permanent.

Pillows with themed panels make wonderful gifts, too. Themes for pillow panels can include birthdays, holidays, the seasons, a high school or college sports team, vacation memories, back to school, and baby showers.

Add interest to a tailored pillow with a contrasting flange. The easy-to-fashion frame accents the size and scale of the pillow without overwhelming the design. Choose an accent or complementary fabric and the trim will truly frame your fabric choice for the pillow's center while linking the accessory visually to the rest of your room's decor.

contrast flange pillow

You can easily adapt the contrast flange to any size or proportion of square or rectangular pillow. The pillow *at left* serves as a lumbar pillow. The same pillow structure can serve as a breakfast pillow for the bed or a toss pillow on the sofa.

A lumbar pillow makes a chair more comfortable because it supports the lower back. Unlike square cushions that press the upper body forward, these shorter cushions allow you to lean back.

Rectangular pillow forms come in a variety of sizes. Choose a height and width that suits the shape of your chair. To customize a pillow size:

• Purchase a pillow form slightly larger than the size you need.

• Work the filling away from a seam.

• Stitch a new seam to change the dimensions of the pillow form.

This technique works best with feather/down pillow forms. This filling is easier to compress and shift inside the cover than polyester fiberfill. Keep in mind that you will have a higher concentration of filling in the resized pillow than in the original. The feel of the pillow will be firmer and heavier.

CUSHIONS FOR COMFORT

■ Add drama and comfort to the design of your dining room with small pillows tucked into the back of each dining chair. The pillows add color, texture, and softness to a room that is typically full of furnishings with hard surfaces, such as wood and glass. At dinner parties, the pillows provide practical comfort for your guests as they linger over coffee or cordials and dessert.

■ In formal dining rooms, indulge in fine fabrics for the front of the pillow. To protect the wood chair backs, use velvet or wool felt for the back panel of the pillow.

■ Choose a small 12"×16" feather/down-filled pillow form for the back of dining chairs. This pillow form is often called a "boudoir" pillow. The size fits nicely into most dining chairs.

materials

Pillow form
54"-wide decorator fabric
54"-wide decorator
   accent fabric
Zipper
Paper

sewing tools

Sewing machine
Iron and ironing board
Fabric marking pen or pencil
Pins
Needles
Thread
Scissors
Tape measure
Liquid ravel preventer

skill level: intermediate
time required: 5 hours

contrast flange pillow:

1 Determine the best size for the pillow and purchase a pillow form in this size. If no form is available, purchase a larger form. Shaking vigorously, move the pillow filling away from the seam that must be moved to create a form of the correct size. Measure and mark the line on the cover. Stitch on the line, then restitch close to the first stitching (see Figure 1). Trim the cover close to the stitching line.

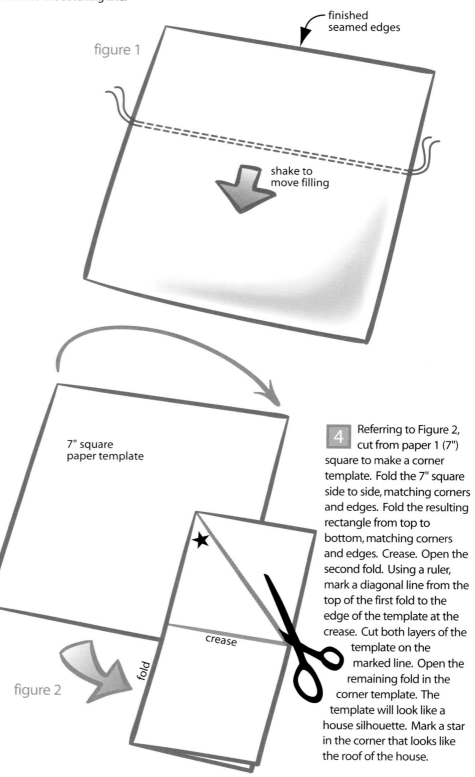

figure 1

finished
seamed edges

shake to
move filling

7" square
paper template

figure 2

fold

crease

★

2 For the cut size of the front and back panels, measure the pillow form from top to bottom and add 1". Measure the pillow form from side to side and add 1". Drape the fabric on the pillow form to find the desired placement of the fabric design. From the fabric, cut 1 front panel and 1 back panel to this size. Set the front and back panels aside.

3 For the cut size of the border, measure the length of each side of the front panel and add 7" to each measurement. From the accent fabric, cut a 7"-wide strip to the required length for each side of the pillow. Arrange the border strips around the front panel with right sides facing up.

4 Referring to Figure 2, cut from paper 1 (7") square to make a corner template. Fold the 7" square side to side, matching corners and edges. Fold the resulting rectangle from top to bottom, matching corners and edges. Crease. Open the second fold. Using a ruler, mark a diagonal line from the top of the first fold to the edge of the template at the crease. Cut both layers of the template on the marked line. Open the remaining fold in the corner template. The template will look like a house silhouette. Mark a star in the corner that looks like the roof of the house.

5 With right sides together and raw edges aligned, stack the right border on the top border, matching the 7"-long edges. Place the corner template on top of the stack, aligning the edges. Place the star corner of the template $1/2$" from the raw edge of the fabric. Mark along the 2 sides of the starred corner to mark the stitching lines for the mitered corner of the border (see Figure 3). Remove the template. Pin the border strips together on the marked line. Stitch on the marked line. Do not backstitch, chain, or otherwise secure stitches at either end of the stitching line. Pivot the stitching at the corner. Trim the seam allowance to $1/2$". Press the seam open. Mark and stitch the remaining corners of the border in the same manner.

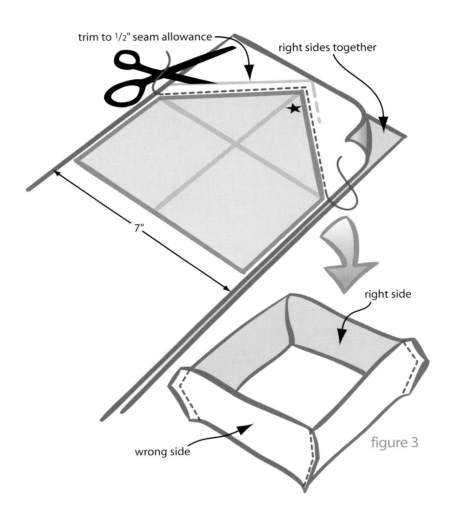

trim to $1/2$" seam allowance

right sides together

7"

right side

wrong side

figure 3

6 When all corners have been stitched, fold the border with wrong sides together. Bring the raw edges of each strip together in the center of the frame-like border. Align the seams at each corner and press the folds. Press the corners flat.

7 With right sides together and raw edges aligned, pin the border to the front panel (see Figure 4). To ease the border around the corners, remove several stitches from the ends of the miter seams. Using a $1/2$" seam allowance and long stitch length, baste the border to the front panel. Pivot the stitching at the corners. Pin the border edges and corners to the center of the front panel.

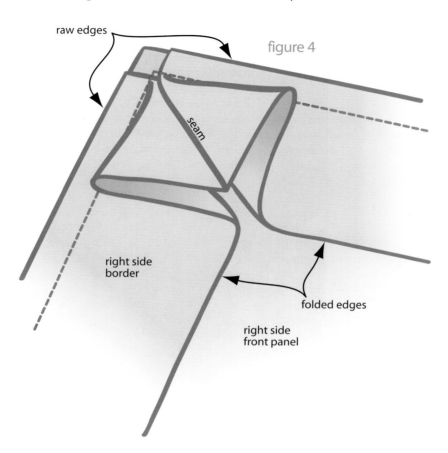

raw edges

figure 4

seam

right side border

folded edges

right side front panel

8 With the right sides together and raw edges aligned, pin the back panel to the front panel over the border. Using a normal stitch length, follow the basting line for the border to stitch the back panel to the front panel. Stitch all corners, pivoting the stitching at the corners. Leave a long opening in 1 side for turning. Grade the seam allowances. Clip the corners of the front and back panels and press the seam.

9 Turn to the right side through the opening. Place the border on the edge. Turn under $1/2$" along the raw edge of the opening and press flat. Insert the pillow form into the cover through the opening. Using a needle and thread, stitch the opening closed by hand.

ribbon flange: Instead of stitching a fabric border, use wide decorator ribbon to frame a pillow.

1 Begin with a ribbon that is at least 3" wide and 12" longer than the total combined length of the template edges (see Step 2).

2 Measure the pillow form from top to bottom and from side to side; add twice the ribbon width less 1" to each measurement. From paper, cut 1 piece this size for a border template. On the border template, use a ruler to draw diagonal miter lines in each corner.

3 On the border template, place the ribbon right side up with the top edge aligned with the template edge. At the corner, crease the ribbon along the diagonal line.

4 Make a 1"-deep tuck in the ribbon at the outside corner; crease the ribbon again along the diagonal line at the corner, and then continue the ribbon along the left edge of the template (see Figure A). Make creases and folds at each corner in the same manner. Lift the ribbon from the template and pin the creases in each corner with wrong sides together.

5 To make small French seams at the corners, stitch parallel to and ¼" from the pinned creases in the tucked portion of the ribbon. Trim the excess ribbon ⅛" from the stitching line. Apply liquid ravel preventer to the cut edges and let dry (see Figure B).

6 Remove the pins from 1 pinned corner crease. Turn the ribbon along the stitching line so right sides are together. Tuck the tip of the corner into the end of the seam, encasing the tip in the seam. Replace the pins along the creases in the ribbon sections. Stitch the seam following the crease. Chain or backstitch the seam at the outer corner, leaving the threads unsecured at the inside corner. Stitch the remaining corners in the same manner (see Figure C).

7 Press the seams. Open the corners. Pin and stitch the ribbon border to the front panel in the same manner as the fabric border.

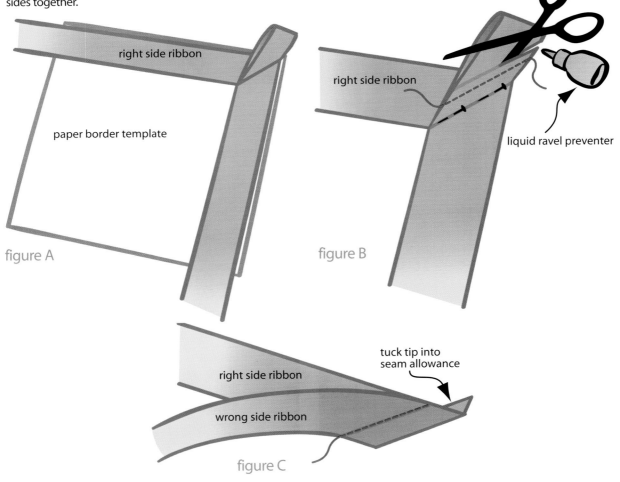

right side ribbon

paper border template

figure A

right side ribbon

liquid ravel preventer

figure B

right side ribbon

wrong side ribbon

tuck tip into seam allowance

figure C

The floor may be the best seat in the house

if you have plenty of big, firmly stuffed cushions like these. For kids watching television or doing homework at the coffee table, floor cushions offer comfortable, versatile seating.

floor cushions

When the floor cushions aren't in use, stack them in a corner—they'll be out of the way but still decorative, adding a splash of color and pattern.

To make floor pillows, look for European standard cushions, which are 26 inches square. Filled with a firm fiberfill or feather/down mix, they make excellent forms for floor cushions.

Choose durable fabrics for the cover and welting. Insert a zipper in one edge of the pillow so you can remove the cover occasionally for cleaning. To preserve the finish and size of decorating fabric, have the covers cleaned by a professional dry-cleaner.

materials

26"-square pillow form
1¾ yards 54"-wide
    decorator fabric
24" invisible zipper
3½ yards fat cord (filler cord)
¾ yard contrast fabric

sewing tools

Sewing machine
Thread
Pins
Needles
Tape measure
Iron and ironing board

skill level: beginner
time required: 3¼ hours

floor cushions:

1 From fabric, cut 2 (28") squares for the top and bottom panels. From contrast fabric, cut 3½ yards of 3½"-wide bias strips for the welting. Stitch the strips together at the short ends. With wrong sides together and long edges matching, fold the bias strip around the cord. Using a zipper foot and long stitch length, baste close to the cord, encasing the cord in the fabric cover.

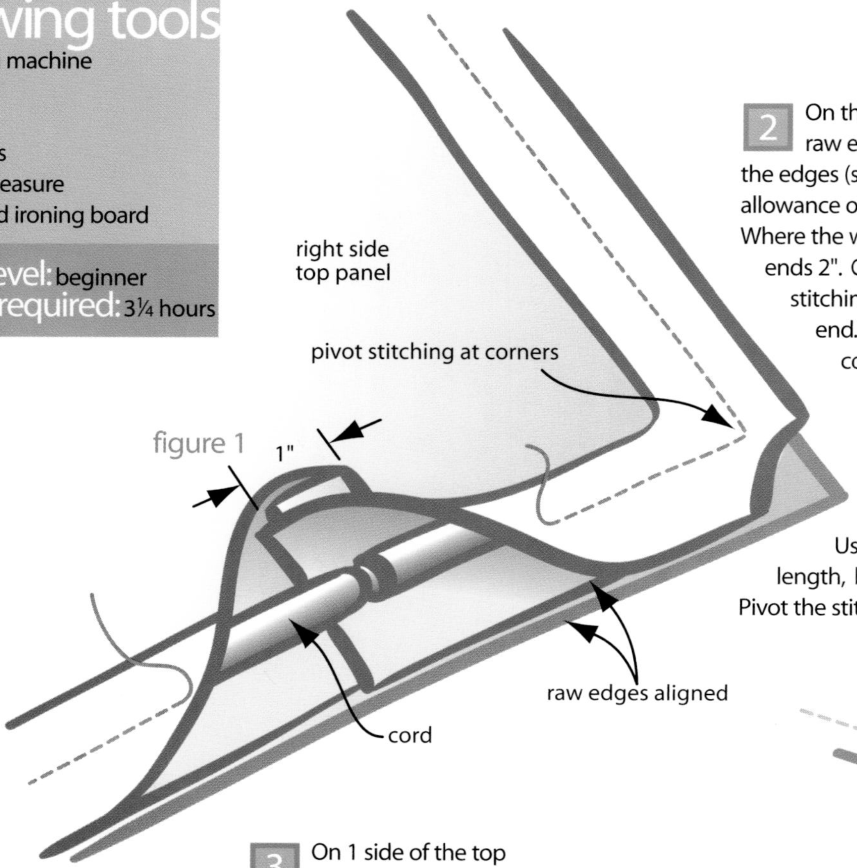

2 On the right side of the top panel, with raw edges aligned, pin the welting to the edges (see Figure 1). Clip the seam allowance of the welting in the corners. Where the welting ends meet, overlap the ends 2". Cut the welting and remove the stitching from the fabric cover on each end. Unfold the fabric and cut the cord ends to meet. Refold 1 end of the cover over the cord. On the remaining end, turn the cover under 1" and refold the fabric around cord, concealing the raw ends of the fabric cover. Using a zipper foot and long stitch length, baste the welting to the top panel. Pivot the stitching at the corners.

right side
top panel

pivot stitching at corners

figure 1

1"

cord

raw edges aligned

3 On 1 side of the top panel, use a zipper foot and regular stitch length to stitch the welting to the top panel along the previous basting. Open the zipper, turn the coils out flat, and press with a warm iron. Center 1 side of the zipper on the seam allowance of the welting on the stitched side (see Figure 2). Place the coils along the stitching line for the welting. Using a zipper foot, stitch the tape to the seam allowance.

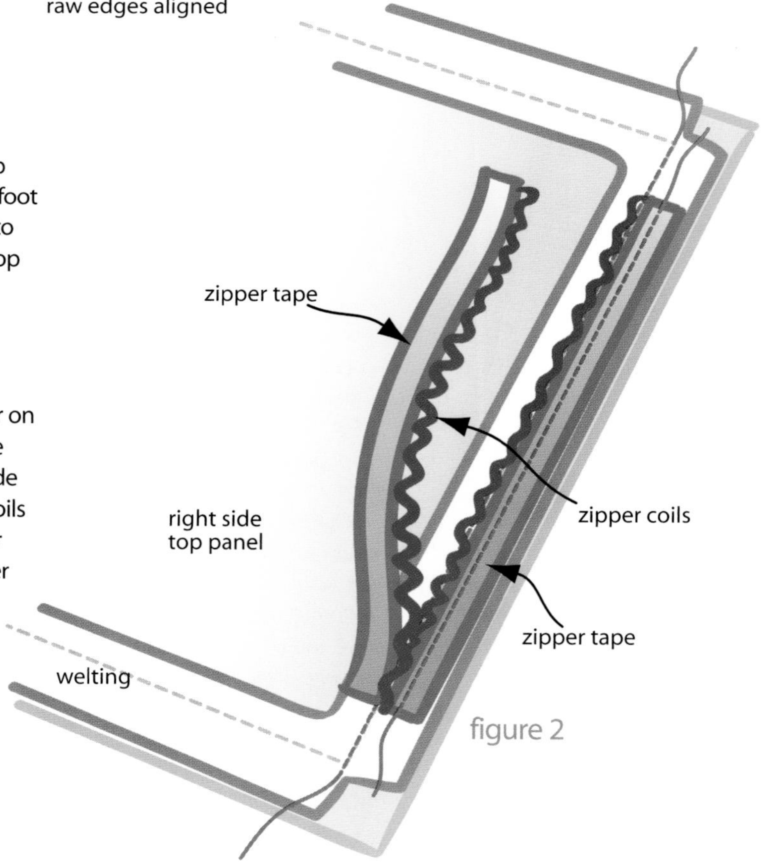

zipper tape

zipper coils

right side
top panel

zipper tape

welting

figure 2

4 Align the bottom panel with the zipper edge of the top panel (see Figure 3). On the right side of the bottom panel, align the zipper tapes with the raw edge. Using the zipper foot, stitch the tape to the panel.

5 With right sides together and raw edges aligned, stitch each end of the seam beyond the zipper, using a zipper foot. Press the seam and open the zipper.

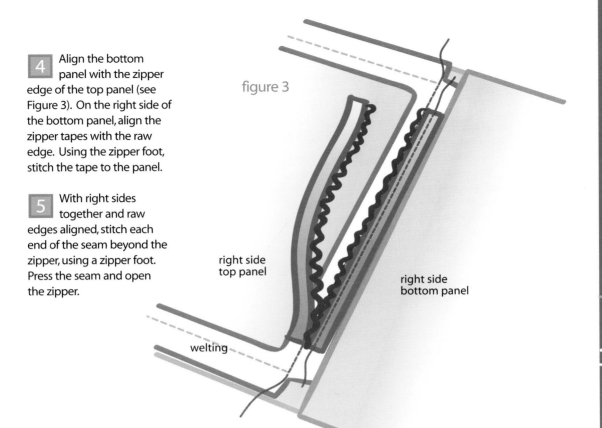

figure 3

right side top panel

right side bottom panel

welting

6 With right sides together and raw edges aligned, pin the top panel to the bottom panel on the remaining 3 sides. Using a zipper foot and regular stitch length, stitch along the previous basting lines. Pivot the stitching at the corners. Grade the seam allowance and clip the corners. Press the seams. Turn the cover to the right side, pulling the welting to turn the corners. Press the seams. Insert the pillow into the cover through the zipper and close the zipper.

FILLER CORD AND FAT CORD

■ Filler cord is a mesh-wrapped fiber tube used to make welting or piping for home decorating projects. The cord is available in a range of closely graduated sizes, from about $6/32$" to $3/8$". The most commonly used size for slipcovers and pillow covers is $6/32$".

Fat cord is a larger version of filler cord. It is also constructed of long cotton-like fibers in a mesh wrapper. Fat cord has a diameter of $3/4$" to 1". It is often used as an exaggerated welting for large-scale pillow covers, upholstery pieces, and the hem edge of table skirts.

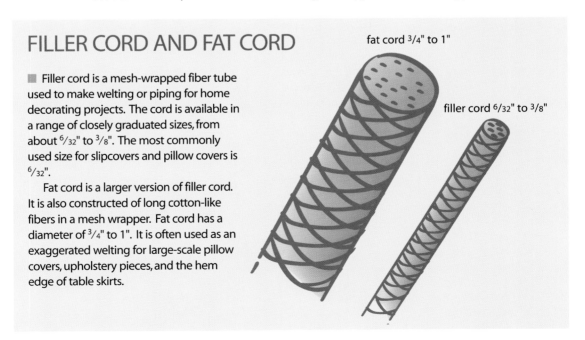

fat cord $3/4$" to 1"

filler cord $6/32$" to $3/8$"

glossary

All-over design: a fabric or wallpaper motif that has no obvious directional emphasis.

Baste: to hold pieces of fabric together temporarily with long, loose stitches, usually made by using the longest stitch length on your sewing machine; basting may be used as a guide for permanent stitches and removed after stitching permanently.

Batting: cotton or polyester padding sold in rolled sheets in a range of thicknesses. Polyester batting is commonly packaged for quilters and is readily available at crafts and sewing shops.

Bias: the diagonal of the weave or a line across the grain of a fabric, drawn at a 45-degree angle to the selvage edge; cloth cut on the bias will stretch, allowing a smoother fit around curves.

Clip: to make snips or tiny cuts into the seam allowance, up to but not through the stitching, so the seam will lie flat. On a concave curve, make triangular notches to allow for flattening the seam easily.

Cord with lip: a type of ready-made upholstery trim featuring a ropelike cord attached to a fabric lip; the lip is installed in the seam so the cord rests on the seamed edge of the item.

Crosswise grain: the weft, or grain of the fabric going across the width of the fabric from selvage to selvage.

Cut length: the measurement of a piece of fabric that includes allowances for hem, header, any gathers or pleats, and fabric repeat; the length to which you need to cut fabric before you begin sewing.

Cut width: the measurement of a piece of fabric that includes allowances for hems, gathers, or pleats; the width to which you need to cut the fabric before you begin sewing.

Directional pattern: a fabric design that has an obvious top or bottom; the direction needs to be considered when placing a pillow pattern on the fabric. Also referred to as one-way design.

Ease: a technique used to distribute two unequal fullnesses of fabric in order to join them in a smooth seam; to curve a trim around a corner, changing a square corner to a rounded one.

Edgestitch: to stitch close to the folded edge of the fabric with medium-length to short stitches.

Facing: a piece of fabric or nonwoven material stitched to the raw edge of fabric and then turned to the wrong side; it produces a stiffer, more substantial edging than simply hemming a raw edge; it is often incorporated into a design to conceal raw edges.

Filler cord: a mesh-wrapped fiber tube used to make welting or piping. Filler cord is available in a range of closely graduated sizes; the most common size for pillow trim is $^6/_{32}$ inch.

Gimp: flat braid or round cording used to trim pillows, curtains, or upholstered pieces.

Grade: to trim the layers of fabric in a seam to different depths in order to eliminate bulk and create a smooth transition from the seam to the outside edge of the seam allowance.

Gusset: in home sewing, a strip of fabric inserted between two panels to provide flexibility; the gusset creates a boxlike side edge between the front and back of the pillow.

Hem: a finished edge; an edge of the fabric that is folded over and stitched. Usually the hem is understood to be the bottom edge.

Hemstitch: worked by hand from the wrong side of the fabric, hemstitching secures a folded edge to the fabric by means of diagonal stitches. Draw the needle through the folded edge from underneath, pick up one or two threads of the flat fabric, then insert the needle in the folded edge and draw it through. Continue in this manner to secure the hem; the stitches should be nearly invisible from the front.

High-density upholstery foam: firm polyurethane foam pads for use in cushions, bolsters, or pillows. Foam pads referred to as high density are resiliant and resist crushing with heavy or prolonged use.

Interfacing: nonwoven fabric, available in varying weights, that is used to stiffen fabric and strengthen seams.

Invisible thread: nylon thread that is clear or smokey in color. When used in the top of the sewing machine, the stitches blend into the fabric.

Lengthwise grain: the grain of the fabric that runs parallel to the selvages.

Lining: a firmly woven, smooth-finish cotton used to back decorator fabric for a smoother, more finished appearance.

Liquid ravel preventer (seam sealant): a clear liquid adhesive applied to the cut edges of fabric or cording to prevent fraying.

Lockstitch: at the beginning or end of a line of stitching, take a few stitches in the same place with the sewing machine.

Notch: on a concave curve, to make triangular clips to allow for flattening the seam.

Paper-backed fusible web: a heat-activated adhesive product that is used to bond fabric to fabric or fabric to other porous surfaces.

Passementerie: a French term for fancy trims such as fringe, braid, cording, and tassels that add texture and color to home decorating projects.

Pillow form: a ready-made cushion in one of a variety of standard shapes and sizes; the filling may be down, feather/down, or polyester fiberfill.

Pivot: leaving the sewing machine needle in the fabric, raise the presser foot, turn the fabric at a sharp angle, lower the presser foot, and continue stitching. Pivoting at corners and points is necessary to make a crisp point on the finished piece.

Pleat: to fold fabric back on itself in a regular pattern at desired intervals to make a trim or a finished design. Also the finished folds made in this way.

Prominent pattern: an obvious motif, such as a large floral bouquet set against a plain background.

Repeat: the vertical length of a design or motif.

Right side: the patterned, printed, or figured side of a piece of fabric. This is the side that is intended to show.

Ruche: a pleated or gathered strip of fabric.

Seam allowance: the fabric between the raw edge and the seam line; usually $^1/_2$ inch in home decorating projects.

Seamline: the line on which you stitch to join two pieces of fabric.

Selvage: the edge of a piece of woven fabric, finished by the manufacturer to prevent unraveling; the selvages are cut off before you begin sewing. Selvages provide information as to the manufacturer, the colors in the fabric, and the direction of the design or pattern repeat.

Spray fabric protector: a chemical spray that may be applied to a fabric to help it repel soil and moisture.

Straight grain: the grain that runs the length of the fabric, parallel to the selvages.

Tack: to secure with a few small hand stitches.

Tassel fringe: a decorative trim that consists of a gimp or braid portion combined with a fringe comprised of tassels.

Tension: the balance between the bobbin and needle threads on a sewing machine; correct tension ensures a perfect stitch.

Topstitch: a line of stitching worked from the right side of the fabric to reinforce a seam and/or to make a decorative effect.

Tuck: a small fold or pleat in a fabric or trim.

Turn under: to turn the edge of a piece of fabric to the wrong side, usually by a prescribed amount, such as 1/2 inch.

Welting: filler cord covered with fabric and used to trim edges or seams.

Wrong side: the back of the fabric, not intended to be seen in the finished project.

Zipper foot: a sewing machine attachment designed for installing zippers; the design of the foot allows the needle to stitch close to items such as zippers and cording.

credits

Waverly products shown in this book were available as of publication date. Please note that items may be discontinued without notice. If a fabric you like is no longer available, call consumer information at 800/423-5881.

Page 6: Design: Rhea Crenshaw, Memphis, TN; photo, Emily Minton; styling, Julie Azar; workroom: Unique Decor, Memphis, TN. Center pillow: Garden Lane 663393; right pillow: Lunette 600965.

Page 12: Styling: Heather Lobdell; photo: Jeff McNamara; accessories: Waverly Home.

Page 16: Design, photo, styling, workroom: see Page 6. Center stripe on pillow: Hanover 661080; check sections: Tate Check 602345; green sections: Arcadia/Boxwood 601459.

Page 22: Design, styling: Catherine Kramer; photo: Hopkins Associates. Walls: Waverly paints WP136 Snow White,

colorwashed with WD303 Lichen. Pillow: 664423; sofa: 664370; solid pillow: Limerick 647106.

Page 30: Design: Michael Buchanan; styling: Cynthia Doggett; photo: Tria Giovan. Checked pillows: Check It Out 664403; Floral Festival 663971; plaid: Picnic 663792.

Page 34: Design, photo, styling, workroom: see Page 6. Wallpaper: Pantry Plaid 570961; window seat cushion and pillow with brush fringe: Charade Vintage 662550; button pillow: Ivy League 662701; flange pillow: Country Fair 662687.

Page 48: Rose medallion pillow: Country Fair 662684, Old Mill Inn Vintage 662172; small pleated ruffle pillow, Abigail 662692, Country Fair 662684.

Page 56: Design: Sally Draughon, Previews Interior Design, Macon, GA; photo: Emily Minton. Bed, shams: discontinued; bed pillows: Parlour Plaid 600723.

Page 64: Design: Dondra Green Parham; construction: Sonja Carmon; photo: Peter Krumhardt. Pillow: Party Plaid 647301.

Page 68: Comforter, shams: Country Life Toile, Waverly Home Fashions; yardage: 659433; neckroll check: McCheck 608025.

Page 74: Designer, photographer, stylist, workroom: see Page 6. Envelope pillow: Cabin Plaid 602422; seat cushion: Westbourne 663670.

Page 78: Design: Elizabeth Dooner; photo: Emily Minton. Round gusset pillow Dominica 600983; white pillows: Admiral 601000; toile pillow: Garden Toile 664572; check pillows: Devon Check 630377; Euroshams: Picnic Check 630266.

Page 84: Pillows: Inga 664032, Baltic Brocade 664052; coverlet, bolsters: Baltic Brocade 664052; pillows, table scarf: Hans 664062, Eugenia 664002; canopy: Greta 664072, Gustavian Stripe 664012; color Oyster. Sheers: Caprice 631302.

Page 90: Design, photo, styling, workroom: see Page 6. Bolster: Ivy League 662701.

Page 91: Design, photo, see Page 78. Bolster: Devon Check 630377.

Page 92: Design, styling: Carla Breer Howard; photo: Jon Jensen. Pillows: Party Plaid 647302; hammock pad: Newstead Sun 'N Shade 664140; workroom: Stoich Designs, Larkspur, CA.

Page 96: Design, styling, photo, see Page 22. Pillow: Old World Linen 645621; button-on panel: Chubby Check 663613; chair slipcover: Ottoman 647020.

Page 100: Ottoman: Stockholm Stripe 647260; chair: Inga 664032; Nicholas Plaid 664022; lumbar pillow, Eugenia 664002; with flange, Hans 664062; color Oyster.

Page 106: Design, styling, photo, see Page 30. Pillows: Jester 600001, Lynnbrook 663721.

index